Series Book Clubs

Lucy Calkins, Series Editor

Amanda Hartman with Colleagues from the Teachers College Reading and Writing Project

Photography by Peter Cunningham

Illustrations by Elizabeth Franco

HEINEMANN ◆ PORTSMOUTH, NH

To Kathy Collins, who reminds us that little readers are ready for big ideas.—Amanda

Heinemann
361 Hanover Street
Portsmouth, NH 03801–3912
www.heinemann.com

Offices and agents throughout the world

© 2015 by Amanda Hartman and Lucy Calkins

All rights reserved. No part of this book may be reproduced in any form or by any electronic or mechanical means, including information storage and retrieval systems, without permission in writing from the publisher, except by a reviewer, who may quote brief passages in a review, with the exception of reproducible pages, which are identified by the *Units of Study for Teaching Reading* copyright line and can be photocopied for classroom use only.

"Dedicated to Teachers" is a trademark of Greenwood Publishing Group, Inc.

The authors and publisher wish to thank those who have generously given permission to reprint borrowed material:

Days with Frog and Toad, by Arnold Lobel. Text copyright © 1979 by Arnold Lobel. Used by permission of HarperCollins Publishers.

Illustrations by Ann Strugnell, copyright © 1981 by Ann Strugnell; "The Pudding Like a Night on the Sea," and "My Very Strange Teeth" from *The Stories That Julian Tells* by Ann Cameron, text copyright © 1991 by Ann Cameron. Used by permission of Random House Children's Books, a division of Penguin Random House LLC. All rights reserved. Any third party use of this material, outside of this publication, is prohibited. Interested parties must apply directly to Penguin Random House LLC for permission. Copyright © 1981 by Ann Cameron. Now appears in *The Stories That Julian Tells* published by Pantheon Books. Reprinted by permission of Curtis Brown, Ltd.

Magic Penny (Love Is Something). Words and Music by Malvina Reynolds © Copyright 1955, 1959 UNIVERSAL–NORTHERN MUSIC COMPANY/MCA Music Limited. Copyright Renewed. All Rights Reserved. International Copyright Secured. Used by Permission. Reprinted by Permission of Hal Leonard Corporation and Music Sales Limited.

Materials by Kaeden Books and Lee & Low Books, appearing throughout the primary Reading Units of Study series, are reproduced by generous permission of the publishers. A detailed list of credits is available in the Grade 2 online resources.

Cataloging-in-Publication data is on file with the Library of Congress.

ISBN-13: 978-0-325-07710-9

Series editorial team: Anna Gratz Cockerille, Karen Kawaguchi, Tracy Wells, Felicia O'Brien, Debra Doorack, Jean Lawler, Marielle Palombo, and Sue Paro
Production: Elizabeth Valway, David Stirling, and Abigail Heim
Cover and interior designs: Jenny Jensen Greenleaf
Photography: Peter Cunningham
Illustrations: Elizabeth Franco
Composition: Publishers' Design and Production Services, Inc.
Manufacturing: Steve Bernier

Printed in the United States of America on acid-free paper
19 18   PAH   5

Acknowledgments

MANY PEOPLE have given their time, energy, and best thinking to help this book come to fruition. Our first thanks goes to our leader and the head writer of this entire project, Lucy Calkins. Thank you for the years of scholarship, teaching, writing, and studying alongside teachers and children. Thank you for your guidance, vision for young readers, and all the words and ideas that you gave to help make this unit rigorous, fun, and inviting for teachers and children everywhere.

This book has more coauthors than can fit onto one cover. It's been a favorite at the Project for a very long time. All the staff developers at the Project have helped to develop the methods and ideas you'll read in this book, as have the teachers and kids who have literally breathed life into it over the years. Warm thanks go to the talented group of colleagues at the Teachers College Reading and Writing Project (TCRWP), in particular, to the primary staff developers. Our study groups, think-tanks, workshops, and curriculum development work over the years have all contributed to this book and the series.

Because the unit has accumulated new insights, tools, tips, and techniques year after year, the challenge when writing the unit was to draw from all those glorious ideas so as to fashion a single pathway. Lots of people helped with that effort. In addition to Lucy, Liz Dunford Franco and Julia Mooney helped, as did Becca Rappaport Sanghvi, Valerie Geschwind, and Julie Steinberg.

A tremendous amount of gratitude goes to the team at Heinemann. Although many people at both Heinemann and the Project have been working into the wee hours of the night and throughout every weekend for a very long time, it is Abby Heim who carries the weight of being ultimately responsible for pulling all the paragraphs, pages, people, and Post-its together so that this Units of Study series comes together into that lovely little box. The baton of this project will soon be passed to the ever-energetic Lisa Bingen and to Stephen Perepeluk, a long-time friend of our organization, and we are grateful in advance for their groundbreaking efforts to bring the units to teachers and principals across the world.

A big thanks to our editors, Sue Paro and Havilah Jespersen, for your impressive attention to this unit. Sue, I know that each of these books requires that a thousand details are brought together just right, and I thank you for making that happen. Havilah, thank you for drawing on a deep understanding of reading development and of young readers as you read over and added to and revised the final draft of this unit.

This is the final book of the K–2 series, and so it seems like a good time to thank all of the people with whom we work at TCRWP who make our work shine. Thank you Judy Chin, Dana House, Beth Neville, Kathy Neville, Sara Johnson, Lisa Cazzola, Shveta Dogra, Chrissy Glaser, Tim Lopez, Jose Baires, Mary Ann Mustac, Gillian Oswald, and Rebecca Godlewicz. Without you, none of this would be possible.

The people who breathe life into this unit are the teachers and students. We would like to thank all the schools who have piloted this unit over the years and who helped us to clarify the ideas that finally made it to these pages. We would like to give special thanks this year to the second-grade teams at PS 59M and PS 503BK for all your help and contributions before, during, and after piloting this work.

—Amanda and the entire TCRWP community

Contents

Acknowledgments • iii

An Orientation to the Unit • vi

BEND I   Becoming Experts on Characters

1. Series Book Readers Collect Information about the Main Characters • 2

In this session, you'll teach students that when readers aim to be experts on a particular series of books, they collect lots of information about the main characters in the series. One way they do this is by previewing the first book, paying close attention to what they learn about the main characters.

2. Series Book Readers Pay Attention to How Characters Respond to Problems • 8

In this session, you'll teach children that readers can learn a lot about a character by thinking about how the character responds to problems.

3. Series Book Readers Notice Similarities in Their Characters across a Series • 16

In this session, you'll teach children that readers look closely for things that are similar in their series books by thinking about what the character always does or how the character usually feels.

4. Series Book Readers Grow to Understand the Characters • 22

In this session, you'll teach children that readers think about the things they have learned about the characters to understand them even better, like experts.

5. Series Book Readers Use What They Know about the Characters to Predict • 27

In this session, you'll teach children that once they come to know the star character of a series well, they can draw on their knowledge of the character's behavior to almost predict that character's next steps.

6. Series Book Readers Learn about Characters from Their Relationships with Other Characters • 33

In this session, you'll teach children that readers get to know the different people in a character's life and compare them to their own relationships so that they to get to know and understand their character even better.

BEND II   Becoming Experts on Author's Craft

7. Authors Paint Pictures with Words • 42

In this session, you'll invite children to join you in a class inquiry. Together, you will explore this question: "What do authors do to paint a vivid picture with words?"

8. Authors Use Precise Words • 49

In this session, you'll teach children that readers pay close attention to the words that authors choose to know what is happening in a story.

9. **Authors Use Literary Language to Make the Ordinary Extraordinary • 56**

In this session, you'll teach children that another craft move that readers notice is the author's use of literary language. Readers notice the words authors choose to make simple things extraordinary, and they figure out what the author really means.

10. **Authors Think about How Whole Stories—and Series—Will Go • 61**

In this session, you could teach children that authors craft more than just the words. They also think about how the whole story—even the whole series—will go. Once readers figure out how one story goes, they can figure out how all the books in that series will tend to go.

11. **Authors Have Ways to Bring Stories to Life • 64**

In this session, you'll teach children that readers listen for author's craft in the words the author uses and look for it in how the author places the words on the page so that they know how to read like storytellers.

12. **Authors Plan Their Story Endings • 71**

In this session, you could teach students to pay attention to story endings because they prompt readers to think about a lesson the author may be trying to teach.

BEND III   Sharing Opinions with the World

13. **When Readers Love a Series, They Can't Keep It to Themselves • 76**

In this session, you'll teach children that part of the joy of reading is sharing what you read with other people.

14. **Planning the Very Best Way to Share a Book • 81**

In this session, you'll teach children that the best way to share a book or series of books that they love is to prepare a wonderful, thoughtful presentation.

15. **Readers Share Books They Love with Friends: A Book Swap • 85**

In this session, you could prepare students to give a series introduction as a prelude to the actual book swap.

16. **Sharing Opinions by Debating • 87**

In this session, you'll introduce the concept of a debate as a way to share opinions about a book.

17. **Celebration: Supporting Reasons with Examples to Strengthen Debate Work • 91**

In this session, you could teach students to support their reasons with examples from the book.

Read-Aloud and Shared Reading

Read-Aloud • 94

Shared Reading • 103

> Registration instructions to access the digital resources that accompany this book may be found on p. xiv.

An Orientation to the Unit

WHETHER YOUR CHILDREN are fans of Horrible Harry or Miami Jackson, Cam Jansen or Froggy, it's almost inevitable that they'll fall in love with recurring characters who find themselves in challenging predicaments again and again and yet exhibit reassuringly predictable behaviors and beliefs. Your second-graders will welcome the opportunity this unit brings to read a lot about a favorite character. Look out, they may even become a bit obsessed!

One reason we love this unit so much is that a familiar series can provide a safe, supportive context for not only daring thinking, but also for breakthrough work with skills. As a series becomes more familiar to your children, their thinking will become bolder and more insightful. Further, across this unit, your students will become far more adept at the foundational skills upon which all fiction readers rely: previewing, envisionment, prediction, monitoring for sense, inferring, and understanding characters and other story elements. Toward the end of the unit, they'll be challenged to take on even higher-level intellectual work, such as comparing and contrasting.

Students are supported not only by the fact that they are reading within a series but also because they are working within supportive social structures. This unit channels students to work in both partnerships and, much to their delight, book clubs. Usually their conversations start as partnership conversations, as partnerships hold each other accountable and provide maximum support for literal understanding of a book. Clubs, then, come later, after readers have had a chance to read with a partner and are ready to grow ideas with a larger group. Two partnerships come together to form a club. The clubs, like the partnerships, study a series together. Children will relish the chance to talk to clubmates about the beloved cast of characters in their shared series, and this sort of talk will extend their thinking. Talking together will help readers to develop bigger ideas than they would develop on their own.

As your children read, read, read within a series, they'll become experts not only on characters but also on the authors.

This unit provides a wonderful context for moving kids forward into slightly more challenging books. The recurring characters in a familiar series will help. Then, too, many of the books that your students will be reading are highly predictable and that predictability can provide support. Then, too, the unit offers a good opportunity for you to help your children work with greater independence to draw on the full repertoire of skills they have learned throughout the year.

In the first bend of the this unit, students will begin reading a series with their partners, collecting information about the stars (main characters) of their books. Who are the stars, how do they feel and behave? What kinds of trouble do they encounter and how do they respond to that trouble? What are these characters' relationships like? As the week progresses and students swap books within their clubs, they'll think and talk together about the similarities and differences that they find across the series.

In the next bend, students will start rereading a book in their series and engaging in inquiry, thinking about the craft the writer uses. To get this going, you might pose a question to your readers, such as, "What do authors do to paint a vivid picture with words?" They will study ways authors use word choice, figurative language, punctuation, and even patterns to construct their series. Students will uncover the craft that the author uses to hook readers into the series and link the books together.

In the final bend, students will begin to innovate and invent ways to share their books with others. They will think about ways to share the series books that they most love with others. At the end of this bend, they will also begin to learn how to have a debate inside their clubs, as another way to share and talk about books.

THE INTERSECTION OF READING DEVELOPMENT AND THIS UNIT

Your second-graders have now blossomed into almost-third-graders, and many of your readers will be tackling L and M books in this unit. Many young readers will be feeling confident, more able now to orchestrate all the sources of information and to get through tough words with increasing ease. However, as has been true throughout second grade, this confidence can also cause children to fall into the habit of whizzing through their reading, not monitoring for sense. In the writing workshop, you need to guard against your children's newfound facility, which might lead them to plop any old words onto the page without thinking. Similarly in reading, you may find that some readers need encouragement to slow down so as to read more closely. This unit provides many opportunities to engage children in looking at the text carefully, thinking about what the text is saying and about how the writer is saying it.

Series books, at this time in your children's second-grade year, can play a special part in your kids' reading development. Series books are highly patterned. Once your kids read one book in a series, they will see how the series goes and can predict what to expect in the others. In Magic Tree House books, for example, everything is the same. Each time Jack and Annie get in the treehouse, read a book, and have an adventure. Jack is scared; Annie is not. Kids can use the schema they've already built to jump right into these texts, unlike in single stories.

Series will also play a special role in your kids' lives at this age not only because there are so many series written at levels L and M but also because this is an age when kids develop obsessions that become part of their identities. Your second-graders love stickers, bracelets, American dolls, hats, or horses—whatever, they want the poster, the shirt, the cards, and the birthday parties. Series books can tap in to your kids' tendency to get hooked on something—and can give them the security of something dependable in their reading lives. Transitions in life are still tough for many of your eight-year-olds, and series books let kids stick with something familiar for a longer period of time. For your readers who are moving into a new level of text, perhaps with some discomfort, series can be a highly supportive way to begin a new level.

The L/M books that many of your children will be reading in this unit will also give them the opportunity to tackle books in which the characters' motivations, their wants, are clear. Your kids are ready to think about stories not just as accounts of things that people do (going to the park, going to the store) but as steps toward a goal, where characters will run into trouble, into a problem, and need to figure out a response. Within another year, the problems that characters encounter will often be beneath the surface and there may be a whole series of problems in a story. Your second-graders will still have some trouble understanding the full complexity of situations—they still see the world mostly in black and white. The series books they'll read in this unit will give your kids opportunities to think about what characters want but without the complexity they will encounter in a year or so.

By the end of second grade, your readers will likely be ready to do some of their own problem solving. When they face conflicts with classmates and friends, it's best, of course, if you don't solve the problem for them, but instead ask them to think about options for solving those challenges. You'll find that your children are not only becoming more adept problem solvers in their lives but also in their reading. Your children should be able to puzzle over reasons why characters do something, and to think about how all that they know so far in a story sets them up to imagine what might happen next. You'll find that your second-graders are more able to know when to use a strategy and why. They're able to approximate the skills of planning their reading lives, planning how they will reread, how they will make their reading work better. This unit will support this budding tendency, helping kids say things like "I'm going to read this like . . ." and "I'm going to be a good partner by . . ." and "I did this because . . . ."

Partners will, of course, play a key role in this unit. Partners will be reading the same book, and will come together to recap the plotlines, to talk about what they are learning about characters, and to share what they noticed about the author's craft moves. Then, after partners have read some parts aloud and discussed their understandings, they will come together in a book club and talk across the series, comparing similarities and differences. It will be important for them to first rehearse and monitor for meaning in a smaller grouping (a partnership). Because members of a club will be reading other books within the same series, the conversations within the club will help readers learn about books before they read them, and this will be supportive. Activating schema in multiple ways is important for young readers and especially for second-graders who may be new to reading chapter books that require multiple sittings to finish.

Finally, at the end of the unit, students will invent ways to share their opinions about books. In writing workshop, your children will be learning to write their opinions about books and characters. In reading, they will swap books within and across a series, and this will give them lots of opportunities to talk together about why they like a book—talk that will undergird the writing they are doing. Students will then, at the very end of the unit, learn how to debate some of their opinions about characters. If you are teaching the writing unit *Writing About Reading* from Units of Study in Opinion, Information, and Narrative Writing, the work they do in reading workshop will feed into their writing work seamlessly.

OVERVIEW
Bend I: Becoming Experts on Characters

You may begin this unit by holding up a few books that represent series, books about characters such as Junie B. Jones, Fly Guy, or Cam Jansen, and saying, "You know a lot about being experts. Some people in this room are experts on making Lego castles. Some are experts on Barbie dolls, on baseball. Am I right? And am I right that you not only collect *stuff*, you also collect *knowledge*. Am I right? Readers, today we start a new unit. In this unit, you are going to become experts on *series* books."

To begin, you'll form clubs of four students each, giving each pair of partners the same title to read. To clarify, in a Pinky and Rex club, two students will each read *Pinky and Rex and the Spelling Bee* while the other two students read *Pinky and Rex Go to Camp*. In this way, you'll support readers to build and monitor meaning as they meet together to discuss the story.

Throughout this bend, you will teach students that the way they look at things in the world is a lot like the work readers do to pay close attention and learn all they can as they are reading. To start off, you make the connection that reading in a series is much like watching a favorite television show. You might say, "When readers read a lot of books in a series, they especially collect knowledge about the characters who are the stars of the series—like in a TV show. Who are the stars of your TV shows?" Kids will be eager to name favorite characters. They know a lot about these stars, and you will help them understand that as they read they will come to know the stars of their books in the same way.

You will help students not just to study their characters but also to study the plot. In most of their series books, characters will run into troubles or problems to which they must respond. You will want to teach students to not just name the problem but also study how the character handles and responds to those problems. This, too, reveals a lot about the character. You might ask students to play an imagination game. You could say, "Close your eyes. Now, imagine it's a hot summer day and you're at the beach. You just bought a triple-scoop ice cream cone. You walk away from the ice cream stand, holding your cone carefully. As you go to take your first lick, the ice cream drops right into the sand! What would you do? Quick, turn and tell your partner." You'll go on to offer the teaching point, "Today I want to teach you that the way a person responds to trouble says *a lot* about who that person is. In real life and in stories, too, the way a person responds to trouble—to a problem—gives you clues as to what kind of person this is."

In a series, one of the great things that students will discover is that the things that they find in one book are often true across the entire series. You will eventually want your same-book partners to swap books with the other partners in the club so as to study and think across texts. You'll coach readers to consider what is the same about the characters across books and about the types of problems they encounter and the ways they have for handling those problems. Your students will inevitably find differences as well as similarities, and all of this can be discussed during club time.

You will want to help students develop ways of talking across books in their clubs. Talking about *one* book can be tricky; now students will be talking about a couple of different stories. You may give them clear steps to follow to conduct a focused discussion. For instance, once a student shares an idea they have, the group could work together to (1) show "proof," or an example in the story, (2) look in another book or story and decide if this is true there, too, and (3) talk about it! Then they can go on to the next idea.

As students really "dig into" their series book and read across the books, you will want to help them not just collect things that they know about the characters and the trouble but also *think* about what they are collecting. It will be important for them to raise important questions about the characters and the plot. You may say, "Have you ever been in a conversation with a whole group of kids, and you look over at your best friend and see that he's looking really upset, or really mad? And for a moment you think, 'Why is he mad?' But then, because this is your best friend, you can think back over everything and say, 'Ohhhh, I bet I know what got him so upset.' *That's* what it means to be a best friend—you *get* the person . . . ." Then you can teach your students that they can come to know a character so well that even if the book doesn't tell what that character is thinking and feeling and why, you just know. You know because you *get* that character.

As students become experts on their series, they'll become more able to anticipate what will happen to characters in the next series book that they read. You'll want children to draw on all they know to ground their predictions in details from previous texts. You will have read several stories about Frog and Toad to them by now, so you'll want to practice this work using these familiar characters. You might even create a scenario with which to practice the strategy: "Say that Frog and Toad and all the other animals of the forest have been invited to go on a ride in this balloon—but here's the deal: they have to go up at the crack of dawn, before it's even light, and it's cold outside. It's late fall and the leaves have fallen off the trees. But if they go, they will have a once in a lifetime opportunity to fly over the trees and water and land below and to see a beautiful sunrise. How do you think Frog will react? What about Toad? Will they take that balloon ride? Turn and tell your partner!" Using all that they know about the characters, students will be able to come up with several possible predictions. Knowing their characters like good friends and family, your students will surely be able to predict the next steps, or reactions, of their characters in their series books as well.

The bend ends with rallying readers to pay attention not just to a single character but also to the relationships that characters have with each other in the series. As children climb toward higher levels of text complexity, their books will feature more and more characters, and these secondary characters will become increasingly more relevant. You'll help students notice and study these characters, too. You might harken back to the idea that reading researchers love to study second-graders—an idea the kids heard about a lot during Unit 3. "If a researcher wanted to watch you and learn about what you are like as a person, do you think we should put a desk at the back of the room, away from everyone, facing the wall, and have you work at that desk for the next few weeks so the researcher could really watch you? Or, do you think that to get to know you, it would be best for the researcher to watch you in your book club and when you are talking with a partner?" Your students will undoubtedly agree that the researcher would learn more by watching them interacting with others. You will want your students to know that they can be those researchers, studying the characters and their relationships across the series. You'll remind students that in order to grow even bigger ideas about the characters, they'll need to pay close attention to the relationships those characters have. "You can't just think about how they are when they are alone; you need to think about how they are with other people."

Bend II: Becoming Experts on Author's Craft

In this next part of the unit, you'll teach students that they can become experts on the *author* of a series, discovering the craft techniques an author uses. This bend will not only help readers read the text more closely, it will also help them consider what an author is trying to show, the tone a scene evokes, and so forth. Just as children discovered patterns across series books, they're bound to discover similar craft moves across books. You may say your students, "You're ready for even *bigger* work. You see, expert readers know how important it is to pay attention not just to what the *character* is doing *in the story*, but also to what the *author* is doing *on the page*—they pay attention to the author's craft."

If you teach using Units of Study in Opinion, Information, and Narrative Writing, your students probably studied Jane Yolen's *Owl Moon* earlier this year, noticing Yolen's choice of words. Children will also have studied words—gloried in words—during earlier nonfiction reading units, so now you can draw on all that focus on words to ask your readers to reread their series books, looking at the author's choice of words. "As soon as you notice a new word, you will want to pause to think, 'What does this word mean?' Remember, you can do a few things: You can read on a bit in your story to see if the author gives you more information about the word. You can think about what kind of word it is and what it is similar to. You can also think about what it looks like and give different examples of the word. Doing this will help you become even more of an expert! It will help you understand *all* the words your series author uses."

After partners share important parts of a book, you can say, "Now, partners, join up with the rest of your club to share those same parts and any new ideas you have. Listen to the language in one another's parts to see if you can say more about that part. Then—and here is the big thing to think about—look into your own book to see if you *too* have a similar part or idea." In this way, you will help readers to go from noticing a craft move in one book to thinking about whether that same move is used repeatedly across a series.

Of course, as students think about the language in their books, they'll notice literary language. If you ask your students, "Have you been noticing literary language in your series?" and your students say no, you will want to show them how shocked you are. You may even pretend to fall backwards in your chair! You'll want to convey to students that it would be absurd for them to learn about literary language in Unit 3 and to not carry that lens with them into the rest of their lives.

Of course, as students study the craft moves that authors have used, they'll look not only at language but also at structure. As they read on in their series, you'll help them notice and talk about how their books "tend to go." Eventually you can channel readers to notice even the punctuation that authors use to bring their character to life. You might say, "Today I want to teach you that readers can *listen* for the magic authors use to help them read like storytellers. Authors use important punctuation and special kinds of print, like italics, bold words and capital letters so that readers will know how to make a book *sound* beautiful."

Bend III: Sharing Opinions with the World

As you move into the final bend in the unit, you will rally children around the idea that part of the joy of reading is sharing books and opinions about books. You might tell children about inventive ways that other second-grade readers have shared what they are reading, suggesting that doing so could, perhaps, spark ideas for them. You could tell them, "This one kid I know came up with an idea to leave little notes for the next reader throughout a book that she loved. She left notes that said things like, 'Here comes a really important part, pay extra attention!' or 'Can you believe it? I totally think this is a bad idea, you?' or 'Why do you think the character did this?'" Your children will invent some of their own ways to share what they are reading.

This will be a good time to share books because by now (if you haven't already) you'll need to rotate children from one series to another. This gives you an opportunity to teach children to give each other an introduction to the series, doing this in ways that recruit each other to be interested in a series. Ham it up a bit, making this celebratory book swap a big deal. You might say, "Today I want to teach you that when you give a gift, you explain how it's special or how it works. You tell the important things. Readers do the same thing when they share books. They tell the important things." Members of a series club can think together about the most important things other readers need to know about a series.

As students transition into reading their new books, you'll want to remind them to look out for what their friends suggested they need to notice about the series. You might say, "As you start reading your new series, be on the lookout not *just* for the things that your friends told you about but also for *other* things that you find interesting as well! Remember, now you too can become an expert in this new series!" Once again, all of this work teaching others about a series will exactly fit with the work children do in *Writing about Reading* from Units of Study in Opinion, Information, and Narrative Writing.

Before the unit comes to a close, you will want to introduce one more powerful way readers share their opinions about what they are reading. How your children will love being introduced to the challenging work of debate! You might say, "Second-graders, I know you all have invented *lots* of ways to share your books. I have *one* more way that I think is really cool. Are you up for it? It's something that fifth-graders do when they read. Do you want me to tell you? After they read, to share about their books, sometimes they *debate!*"

When teaching children debate work, you'll want to teach the skills of determining importance, supporting reasons with examples, collecting evidence from the text, and working together to make arguments strong. You'll also support your students in skills such as taking turns and using etiquette. In the culminating celebration, you will remind children to give reasons *and* examples. You can nudge them to come to a consensus, saying, "Just like books have endings and units have endings, talks should have endings, too. Decide together on a way to bring your debate to a close. You might take turns repeating your opinion. You might list back your reasons. You might even shake hands!"

ASSESSMENT

Conduct running records to establish new goals for moving your students forward.

In this unit of study, you will want to conduct running records, both formal and informal, looking out for students who are ready to move levels. Many students in the spring will be ready for a new text level, and you will want to be sure to move students as soon as you see signs of readiness. Reading in a series is a great support for students moving up into a new level, so finding out who is ready to move and what skills students need to work on in order to move will be a great priority. Many second-graders by March are reading early chapter books, at or near levels L/M. The end-of-year expectation for second-graders who entered the year on grade level is to exit at a level M. Many students may move beyond into level N, as well. As the year draws to a close, it will be especially important to think about whether your students are on track to make a year's growth (and possibly more for the students who entered below the benchmark).

Gather more information about your students, who are becoming more proficient and fluent readers.

You will want to refer to your spelling inventory to see how students' phonics knowledge is growing, as well as check their growing knowledge of high-frequency words. By spring, most second-graders who are reading at a benchmark reading level have mastered all of the suggested high-frequency words on the word lists we mention in Chapter 6 of *A Guide to the Reading Workshop, Primary Grades*. If you still have students working on reading these words with automaticity, this will be important small-group instruction. In order to move up the ladder of text complexity, students need to be able to integrate the sources of information. Spelling and high-frequency words may be areas to strengthen if you are finding students are in need. You can also refer to Chapter 6 to find these assessments, as well as how to administer them.

Collect data on comprehension skills.

You may decide to do a quick initial assessment of your kids' comprehension skills to help you focus your teaching on what your readers need. You may decide you want to assess how your students think about characters or about the lessons the characters have learned. You could read aloud a short story and prompt your students to stop-and-jot in two or three places to capture a sample of their ideas about characters: how they act or behave, how they have changed, and lessons they've learned. You can then look across students' jottings and study their responses and think about which responses are more sophisticated and inferential and use more of the text, and which ones are more literal and use less of the text. You may want to set new goals for the whole class, individual, and small-group work that you would like to do over the next six weeks.

At the end of the unit, you can conduct a similar assessment to measure how your students have grown. Your second assessment can pose the same questions you asked at the beginning of the unit, using either the same text or one that is similar and at the same level of text complexity.

As the unit unfolds, you may want to gather additional information about how your students think as they read. During read-alouds, as well as during individual conferences, investigate whether children are making better predictions and are drawing on details across a series to inform their thinking. By now, they should be able to make inferences about the characters and to link characters' wants with their problems. Students should read expecting that characters will face challenges and learn lessons. Hopefully, they are relying more on the text and less on the pictures when they look for evidence to support their thinking.

Assess students' reading volume and stamina.

Not only will you want to check running records, spelling inventories, high-frequency word lists, and comprehension skills, but you will also want to monitor students' volume and engagement during reading workshop and at home. As you teach various strategies and content in phonics, students need to apply, re-apply, and transfer these skills and strategies across texts. If reading volume and stamina is low this will impact readers' development greatly. You will want to pay especially close attention to the volume, stamina, and engagement levels of your students who are reading below the benchmark. If students aren't reading enough each day, it will be nearly impossible for them to grow as readers.

Use your assessment data to plan your curriculum.

If you find that a group of your second-graders are reading well below the benchmark during this unit, then you may want to refer to the book *If . . . Then . . . Curriculum: Assessment-Based Instruction, Grades K–2* as a resource for lessons to support your struggling readers. You might choose to pull from the alternate units "Readers Get to Know Characters by Performing Their Books" (for children reading levels D–G) or "Studying Characters and Their Stories" (available in the online resources) alongside this series book club unit as small-group work, or you might select particular lessons or bends to extend your whole-class teaching in this unit.

At the end of this unit, you might consider teaching the *If . . . Then . . . Curriculum: Assessment-Based Instruction, Grades K–2* unit titled, "Reading and Role Playing: Fiction, Folktales, and Fairytales." This unit is geared toward levels J–M. You may find that your second-graders could use more experience with a variety of genres, or that they could benefit from a focus on reading with drama and expression. Often, when children have been reading extensively in just a few series, they aren't getting as much practice with a range of author's styles and different types of stories. Though there are many benefits of series reading, you may find that after lots and lots of it, students might benefit from some practice with starting fresh books, where the characters are brand new and the setting is unfamiliar. You might also turn to this unit for support with teaching kids to think more deeply about the lessons in stories and to think critically about the books they read.

Whether this is your final unit, or you plan to teach one of the alternate units from the *If . . . Then . . . Curriculum: Assessment-Based Instruction, Grades K–2* book, you'll want to create a system for saving your data from one year to the next, so that you can use this year's end-of-year information to help you plan for next year. This will help you to budget your time wisely each year, leaving approximately six weeks per unit, and teaching six to eight units per year. Some teachers also create an at-a-glance sheet for the end of the year to pass up to next year's teacher: a simple class list, with space for each child's final reading levels, spelling stages, and other helpful information.

GETTING READY

Put together a library that can sustain series book clubs.

Children will need to be reading a shared series within a book club. Hopefully at the start of the unit, children within a club can read in same-book partnerships. That is to say, if there are four children in a club, two of the children will be reading one book in the series and the other two students will read a different book from that same series. After a couple of days, the partners will swap and read one another's books. Then they will continue on, reading any other book that is in the series. This means readers will need access to several books within the series. Readers who read beyond benchmark levels (N or above) may all read the same book in the series at the same time, if possible, thus you'll need four copies of each book. Students below benchmark would benefit from having up to ten different titles from the same series, if possible, each week. If this is not possible, you'll need to orchestrate things so that students switch into a new series once they've essentially run through all available books within a series.

To make all of this work, you may need to stagger the time of the day at which kids in other classes in the grade are reading so that you can share resources with other teachers. Here are some suggested series:

Levels L/M (readers at benchmark)

- Magic Treehouse, Cam Jansen, Junie B Jones, Horrible Harry, Pinky and Rex, Ready Freddy, The Polk Street Kids, Miami Jackson, Poppleton, and Jamaica

Levels D–K (readers below benchmark)

- Frog and Toad, Iris and Walter, Fluffy, Little Bear, Danny and the Dinosaur, Mr. Putter and Tabby Cat, Biscuit, Little Critters, Fly Guy, and the Brand New Readers Series

Levels N–P (readers above benchmark)

- The Stories Julian Tells, Secrets of Droon, A–Z Mysteries, Jigsaw Jones, The Zack Files, Amber Brown, The Amazing Monty, Ivy and Bean, Ramona Quimby, and Encyclopedia Brown

Match the texts with the reading skills your students are working on.

As your students approach the end of the year, you will see that their foundational skills are falling into place. That is to say, on a first read of a Magic Tree House book, you will hear your students making better attempts at reading in longer phrases and using proper intonation most of the time as they read. When they try to figure out new or tricky words, you will find that most of the time they are not stymied, but rather use a few strategies to solve the word and think about what it means. In the books that students are reading, they can count on finding new vocabulary as well as figurative language.

Select and gather books and texts for minilessons and guided reading.

As you gather books for guided reading, you will want to find series books or books with short stories that will be just a level above your students' just-right book levels to use in your minilessons. There are advantages to choosing a text that is written at an accessible level, though—each story within the series will be especially brief, which will allow you to quickly get into showing the work that a series reader does. We chose *Days with Frog and Toad* because the book has short episodic chapters, which makes it easier to discover similarities and differences across a series, and because it is written by a literary giant, Arnold Lobel. You might also choose a book at students' benchmark level such as a Magic Tree House book, which has the advantage of being a popular, highly engaging series.

In guided reading groups, you may call children's attention to passages within a novel. For example, Chapter 2 of *The One in the Middle Is a Green Kangaroo* by Judy Blume tells about Freddy wanting to be in a play. Over two pages, his emotions change repeatedly because of situations related to whether or not he can be selected for a part. In the end, he plays the role of a green kangaroo. So, over a three-page spread of less than 200 words, you can design a small-group lesson to determine if your students can recall the events in sequence and why each event might make Freddy feel a certain way.

Select a series for your read-alouds.

If possible, we suggest you select your read-aloud books with varied criteria. You will want to read aloud a series that is short and readable. You may decide to choose a text that is a notch above the end-of-year benchmark, such as *The Stories Julian Tells* by Ann Cameron (level N). That book contains a series of short stories on which students can easily do some compare-and-contrast work. Students will learn about the troubles that Julian and his brother Huey get into together. There are other secondary characters—at the end, Gloria, Julian's new best friend, is introduced. She becomes a recurring character in other books within that series.

Choose other types of read-aloud books to read during this unit of study.

You may also want to read a couple of books in a series that is similar to what your students are reading, such as My Father's Dragon or Pinky and Rex books. Or you might even choose a series that is well above children's independent reading levels, reading from either the Ramona books or the Clementine series. By scaffolding a more complex text through reading aloud, you give children opportunities for higher-level thinking. In this way, you support their understanding of more complex texts and model close reading—a skill you will want them to transfer to their independent reading and to club time. This will require students to think strategically about what they have learned in one text and to transfer that work appropriately to other texts.

Use the read-aloud plan at the back of this book to prepare for one read-aloud across a couple of days as well as others across the unit.

You will find a three-day plan for the read-aloud at the back of this book, using the first two stories in *The Stories Julian Tells* by Ann Cameron. You will find, much like in the previous units, transferable prompts that you can use throughout the book. Simply place the Post-its on the pages indicated, and the Post-it will remind you of exactly what and how to prompt the students. You will find that you then can take these Post-its out and reuse them, not only further along in *The Stories Julian Tells* but in other books as well. You will find that that the skills you are developing here parallel the work that you are doing in the unit of study.

Use the five-day plan in the back of this book to help you prepare for shared reading.

After the read-aloud section, there is also a shared reading section that will not only help you plan a week of shared reading in one text but is also a template to use across this unit of study to help you support and develop the foundational skills your students need in these more complex texts. While fluency and word solving will still be something you will want to support, you will also want to continue working on vocabulary development and working through the literary language in books. You may decide to choose an excerpt of a text or a short story to use as your shared reading for this unit. You will find a five-day plan for the short story, "My Very Strange Teeth," that we selected from *The Stories Julian Tells*. After following the plan we outline, you can continue to follow the template and highlight the types of skills we suggest by transferring our plan to other texts of your choosing.

ONLINE DIGITAL RESOURCES

A variety of resources to accompany this and the other Grade 2 Units of Study for Teaching Reading are available in the Online Resources, including charts and examples of student work shown throughout *Series Book Clubs*, as well as links to other electronic resources. Offering daily support for your teaching, these materials will help you provide a structured learning environment that fosters independence and self-direction.

To access and download all the digital resources for the Grade 2 Units of Study for Teaching Reading:

1. Go to **www.heinemann.com** and click the link in the upper right to log in. (If you do not have an account yet, you will need to create one.)
2. **Enter the following registration code** in the box to register your product: RUOS_Gr2
3. Under **My Online Resources**, click the link for the **Grade 2 Reading Units of Study**.
4. The digital resources are available under the headings; click a file name to download.

(You may keep copies of these resources on up to six of your own computers or devices. By downloading the files you acknowledge that they are for your individual or classroom use and that neither the resources nor the product code will be distributed or shared.)

Becoming Experts on Characters

BEND I

Session 1

Series Book Readers Collect Information about the Main Characters

IN THIS SESSION, you'll teach students that when readers aim to be experts on a particular series of books, they collect lots of information about the main characters in the series. One way they do this is by previewing the first book, paying close attention to what they learn about the main characters.

GETTING READY

- Make sure both members of each reading partnership have a duplicate copy of an unfamiliar book from the series that the partnership will be studying. Ensure you have a lot of books from within that series (see Connection).
- Select several books to hold up as examples of series books (see Connection).
- Choose a demonstration text from a series to use throughout the bend, and be ready to display the first chapter using a document camera or other means. Choose an especially well-written book, one with just a few characters. We suggest *Days with Frog and Toad* by Arnold Lobel (see Teaching and Active Engagement).
- Create a new anchor chart, titled "Series Readers Become Experts on Characters," including the strategy "Collect information and ideas about the main character(s)" (see Link).
- Distribute Post-its to children to mark their stop-and-talk spots (see Link).

MINILESSON

CONNECTION

Launch the unit by pointing out that there is a familiar feel to this, the start of the fourth unit. It's rather like starting a book within a reading series—you have a sense of what to expect.

"Readers, today we start a new unit. In this unit, you are going to become experts on *series* books." I held up a few Junie B. Jones books, a few Fly Guy books, a few Cam Jansen books. "You know a lot about being experts. Some people in this room are experts on making Lego castles. Some are experts on Barbie dolls, on baseball. Am I right?"

"So experts: tell me. What do you do as experts?"

I let the question hang there for a moment. "Do you collect stuff about your topic—like do you collect Legos and baseball stuff?" The kids nodded, thinking of their collections. "And am I right that you not *only* collect *stuff*, you also collect *knowledge* about that stuff? Am I right?" The kids agreed.

Name the teaching point.

"Today I want to teach you that when readers become an expert on series books—when they read a lot of books in a series—they especially collect knowledge about the characters who are the stars of the series."

TEACHING AND ACTIVE ENGAGEMENT

Explain that reading a series is like watching a series show on TV, highlighting that in both instances children become experts on the star of the series. Set up the work of the bend.

"The stars? That sounds like a TV show, doesn't it? Who are the stars of your TV shows?" The kids called out Casey Undercover, Jessie, Phineas and Ferb, and so forth. "Do you know a lot about those guys? About Scooby-Doo or Casey or Jessie or whoever is the star of the show you watch?" The kids nodded, as did I.

"Readers, reading a lot of books in a series is a lot like watching your favorite TV show. Just like you get to know the stars of those TV shows really well, you also get to know the stars of your reading series really well. And to do that, you read with extra intensity.

"Let's try reading a book from a series together. I've chosen the Frog and Toad series by Arnold Lobel. We're not just going to read *Days with Frog and Toad* in a casual way," I mimed tossing the book aside. "We're going to read like experts, and that means we need to collect knowledge and insights, right from the start! I'm going to take a sneak peek and then read the first page or two. Watch so you can do the same things with *your* series book. Ready?"

I placed the book under the document camera to give the class a chance to study the front and back covers. "To become an expert, we need to collect knowledge about the characters," I said, drawing my finger around the cover, to show that I was already doing the work. Then I said, "While you study these characters, I will as well. If you agree with what I say about them, show me by putting your thumb on your knee."

I ran my finger around the illustration on the cover. "So, what I am discovering, right from the front cover, is that Frog and Toad are spending time together. They look like they are about to fly a kite together. And the title is *Days with Frog and Toad*. I wonder if these two friends spend every day together. Hmmm. I know that many of you may already know these characters. Use that to help you collect more information." I turned back to the class, "I see thumbs up! Are those the same kinds of things you were thinking, too?" Several students nodded.

"Let's check the back of the book for more clues to collect more information and grow more ideas about these two characters!" I flipped the book over and invited the class to read the blurb along with me:

> Frog and Toad enjoy spending their days together. They fly kites, celebrate Toad's birthday, and share the shivers when Frog tells a scary story. Most of all, they have fun together—every day of the year.

I prompted partners to do some more noticing and wondering by turning and talking.

Debrief in ways that highlight the replicable work you have done reading the front cover and the back cover blurb, while collecting information and ideas about the characters.

After a minute, I paused their conversation. "Think about what we have done so far to become experts on the stars of our series. We really studied the picture on the cover, and we noticed the title, *Days with Frog and Toad*. This helped us

---

Calling to mind favorite TV shows and cartoons will undoubtedly pique kids' interest. Children will easily describe the stars of these programs and you'll use this to make a strong connection to the work readers do to get to know the main characters of books.

You'll notice that we chose the Frog and Toad series by Arnold Lobel, not only because it is well written and highly engaging but also because each chapter is a vignette and you'll be able to easily study the characters across stories to learn more and discover patterns. This would be more time-consuming work in a longer, continuous chapter book.

Remember that your aim is not to learn all that you can about Frog and Toad, but rather, you're teaching students a replicable process for previewing their texts to collect information and grow ideas about the characters right from the start. Narrate your process as you demonstrate these steps.

SESSION 1: SERIES BOOK READERS COLLECT INFORMATION ABOUT THE MAIN CHARACTERS

to get some ideas going like, 'I wonder if these two characters spend every day together?' We then studied the back cover blurb and did some more noticing and wondering."

Channel children to do similar work with the first few pages of the class book, collecting information about what the characters do often and what they are like.

Then, I moved on to find out more. "Let's read the first few pages and see what else we can find out about Frog and Toad. This time, I'm going to ask you to do all the thinking." I read the first few pages of the first chapter, "Tomorrow," aloud, before pausing to give children a chance to collect the details. "Hmm, so what information have we gathered so far? Turn and collect information about Frog and Toad. List across your fingers all the things you are learning about our star characters. What are they like? What do they like to do? What other information have you collected?"

The children talked and then I chimed in. "I agree with everything you are saying. We know Frog and Toad are best friends and they like to spend their days together doing things like flying kites, celebrating birthdays, and even telling scary stories. And we learned things that they like to do AND what they *don't* like to do. We learned that Toad doesn't like cleaning. He's feeling upset and lazy. I heard some of you say that maybe Frog is trying to help him. You already started learning about their feelings and how they handle problems."

Debrief in ways that highlight the replicable work that students can do whenever they start a new series.

I closed the book, and recapped the process the children had taken to preview the book to get to know the main characters. "Did you see how we got ourselves ready to read, learning as much as we could about the main character, right from the start? We used the front cover and the back cover and we read a bit of the story, pausing to collect information and ideas about the main characters. Readers do that every time they start a new series."

LINK

Set up the work readers will do with partners, and clubs, across the week. Then remind children to preview their books to learn about the main character(s) right from the start.

"So, readers, I know that in your baggie you and your partner both have copies of the same book from the series you'll be studying. And actually, for most books, there are four kids—two partnerships—that will be reading a book in that series. So that means there will be four Pinky and Rex readers, and we're going to call you The Pinky and Rex Club. And there will be four kids reading Junie B. Jones books—so you are the Junie B. Jones club. And so on. We will have lots of series clubs in this class.

"*But* you don't meet as a club yet. You have to get ready for the first club meeting! The way you'll get ready is that you and your partner will read your shared book *really* well, collecting information and ideas about the star of your book. Then, when you are truly experts on your character, you can have a big club meeting.

Notice that the sort of things you highlight tend to be the everyday things: what the characters do often, what they seem to be like. This is the kind of information you'll want your readers to be collecting to piece together an understanding of a character. In upcoming sessions, you'll help students think about these observations in more sophisticated ways. While you may not have heard kids saying all the things you recap in your summary, take this opportunity to deliberately guide your readers toward the work you want them to be doing.

"So right now, open up the book you chose to read first in your series. Let me see you use everything you learned today about how readers become experts on a character. Before you get started reading, remind each other about what you learned that series readers do to become experts on the stars of their series. Then, turn and list what you learned."

As the kids recapped what they'd learned, I revealed a Post-it chart with that also recapped the message from the day.

ANCHOR CHART

Series Readers Become Experts on Characters
- **Collect information about the main characters.**

"So, readers, as you get started today, and every time you start a new series, it's important to learn as much as you can about the characters who are the stars of your series. Get started doing that work now, while sitting right here. I'm going to come around and give you some Post-its while you work. You can use these to flag the things you are noticing to help you collect information about your star characters. The places you mark will be great parts to talk about with your partners." As children got started, I moved among them, sending them back to their reading spots once their work was well underway.

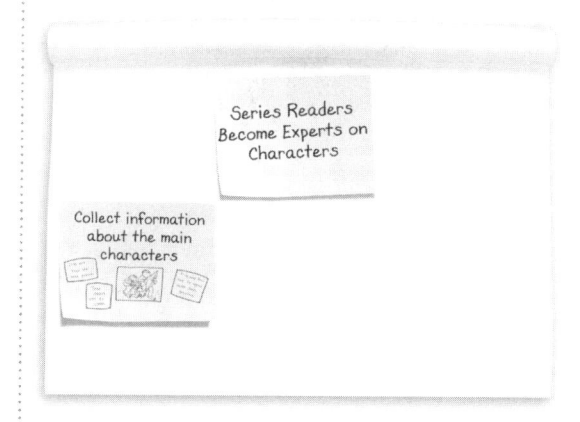

CONFERRING AND SMALL-GROUP WORK

Establishing the Work of a New Bend

AS ALWAYS, the first days of a unit are an opportunity for you to issue a generous invitation to kids, inviting them into the exciting new work of the unit. Certainly the first thing you'll need to do is to make sure the logistics are in place. Do your students realize, for example, that when they have duplicate copies of a book, it means that they do not sit side by side and do choral readings of the book? Instead, you'll expect your readers to read silently, marking parts as they read in preparation for their conversation during the share. Of course children reading at lower levels may need more support to develop their stamina and maintain comprehension. You could have these partnerships set markers to read up to and then pause to talk at these points, giving them multiple opportunities to talk with their partners each day.

You will certainly find children who fly through the pages of their books, and you'll want to encourage them to pause to note what they are observing. You might say, "I notice you are flying through these pages, and it is great to know you can read that way, fast and furious—I often read that way myself. But actually, this unit is asking for a more thoughtful, more alert sort of reading. Like you can run down a trail in the woods, or you can walk with a magnifying glass, seeing the tiny flowers growing in the mossy patch. This unit is asking for more of the second kind of a journey." You may need to do some voiceovers to get your message out to the whole class.

Encourage students by giving little pep talks about reading series books.

Once you have taken care of messaging the really important ways in which you hope children are oriented toward the work of the unit, you will probably find that one of the most powerful things you can do is to be a mentor, demonstrating the sort of attentive, thoughtful, observant reading that you hope your students will be doing. Pull your chair up to a partnership of children, note the book they are reading, and then register delight over their choice of a series. "You are so lucky! Your series is Cam Jansen. I don't know if you know this, but a lot of *third* graders study Cam Jansen. They do that because in third grade kids study mysteries, and—I'm not sure if you realize it—this is a really famous mystery series. So third graders read this book and think whether they can solve the mystery before Cam Jansen does. It is so cool that you are studying this series in *second* grade. Your third-grade teacher will be so surprised when you walk into her class, already an expert on mystery books."

Being able to give little pep talks like that will pique your students' interest in a series. You might want to give introductions to each series. For example, you might sit beside a club and say, "One thing you may not know yet about Magic Tree House books is that in every book Jack and Annie travel not just to a different *place* but also to a different *time*. They often travel back in time to visit important moments in history. The coolest part is you not only learn about the characters but you also learn a bit about history!" Do the same to introduce the key elements of other series, such as spotlighting who the characters are, to support comprehension. For example, you might say, "This is Pinky. He's the boy here." Point to the illustration. "And his best friend is Rex. She's here." So often, children will confuse characters as they read, breaking comprehension of the story and the series. However, you won't want to frontload every key detail of the series, because this will be important work for readers to practice across the unit.

MID-WORKSHOP TEACHING **Growing Ideas from Post-its**

"Readers, I'm glad to see that many of you are flagging things you notice about your main character. Will you get yourself accustomed to not only collecting observations but to also growing ideas about those observations? You might put your Post-it at a part of the story where you see something interesting, but then on the Post-it, you don't have to write just what you see. For example, if you notice Cam Jansen is always saying 'Click,' you could put a Post-it on that part of the book. But you don't need to write the same thing on your Post-it! Instead, you can write what that makes you think. You could write, 'I wonder if __' or "Maybe she does this because __' or 'I think she's always __.'

"Keep reading, keep collecting observations—and keep growing ideas."

SHARE

Sharing Discoveries with Partners

"I KNOW that whenever I watch an episode of my favorite show, I just can't wait to talk to someone else who watched it. I talk about the parts I remember most or the parts that made me think or wonder something. But, I especially want to talk about the star characters.

"Right now, you'll meet with your partner. The best part is, you've both been reading the same book in your series, and working so hard to become an expert, learning as much as you can about the character in your series. One thing you can now do together is share the discoveries you've made! Think about what you have learned so far about the characters, turn to those parts, reread a little together, then work together to name everything you notice."

FIG. 1–1 In these jottings from book club members reading the Frankly Frannie series by A. J. Stern, students collect ideas about the main characters and then discuss these ideas to help them build deeper meaning.

SESSION 1: SERIES BOOK READERS COLLECT INFORMATION ABOUT THE MAIN CHARACTERS

Session 2

Series Book Readers Pay Attention to How Characters Respond to Problems

IN THIS SESSION, you'll teach children that readers can learn a lot about a character by thinking about how the character responds to problems.

GETTING READY

- Ask children to bring their book baggies, Post-its, and a pen or pencil to the meeting area (see Connection, Teaching and Share).

- Display the anchor chart, "Series Readers Become Experts on Characters" and be ready to add the strategy—"Pay attention to how characters respond to problems" (see Connection).

- Prepare to reread the first few pages in the first chapter of the demonstration text. We suggest "Tomorrow," the first chapter of *Days with Frog and Toad*. Be ready to continue reading the chapter (see Teaching).

- Place a Post-it in the part of the text where the character encounters a problem (see Teaching).

MINILESSON

CONNECTION

Ask kids to imagine themselves in a quick succession of problems and to think about how they would react in each scenario.

As children convened in the meeting area, I reminded them to bring not just their book baggies but also Post-its and a pen or pencil. "Now that you are such grown-up readers, will you always bring Post-its and a pen?" I said. "That way if you want to do some writing, you can."

Once the children were settled, I said, "Let's play a little imagination game. Ready? Close your eyes. Now, imagine it's a hot summer day and you're at the beach. You just bought a triple-scoop ice-cream cone. You walk away from the ice-cream stand, holding your cone carefully. As you go to take your first lick, the ice cream drops right into the sand! What would you do? Quick, turn and tell your partner." I leaned in to listen to a few exchanges.

"Okay, here's another one. Imagine you're at the playground with your best friend and he's getting picked on by a big kid. Your friend starts to cry and tells you he wants to go home. What would you do? Turn and tell your partner."

After giving children a brief time to discuss their reactions to that problem, I set up another scenario. "Okay, last one. Imagine you're at the mall with your mom and there are people everywhere! Suddenly, you can't find your mom. You're lost! What would you do? Turn and tell your partner."

Begin the drumroll that sets up your teaching point for the day.

I called students back together and said, "There are many different ways a person can respond to a problem. When your ice cream falls in the sand, you can have a tantrum. Or you can say, 'Is there any way I could get another? Maybe if I tell the ice-cream man what happened I can convince him to give me another.' Or you could scoop up the top part of the ice cream—the part that didn't get into the sand—and eat just that part. Here is my point."

❖ Name the teaching point.

"Today I want to teach you that the way a person responds to trouble says *a lot* about who that person is. In real life and in stories, too, the way a person responds to trouble—to a problem—gives clues as to what kind of person this is."

I added the strategy to the chart.

> **ANCHOR CHART**
>
> Series Readers Become
> Experts on Characters
>
> - Collect information about the main characters.
> - **Pay attention to how characters respond to problems.**

Pay attention to how characters respond to problems

Ensure the scenarios you describe in this connection are quick: boom, boom, boom. One, the next, the next. Don't belabor this and don't turn this into an invitation for a whole-class discussion. You are trying to set kids up to have an aha moment in which they realize that the problems a person encounters in life require a response, and the response reveals a lot about that person. The work you want kids doing now doesn't call for a whole-class discussion—and you don't have time for that.

TEACHING

Teach students to notice how a character responds to a problem and figure out what that response tells about the character.

"Will you and your partner get out your series book?" After children had their books out of their baggies, I said, "Will you look over what you have read so far and talk about whether there is a place in the story where your main character runs into a problem? See if you can find that part, and put a Post-it on it."

After giving them a moment to do this, I pressed on. "I have a Post-it in our Frog and Toad book, because when we left off reading yesterday, we knew one problem, right? Toad's home was a mess and he was feeling grumpy and tired. So, I want you to watch what I do to notice how the characters in this book respond to trouble, to a problem. Then in a moment, you can think about how the characters in *your* book respond to trouble. You ready?

"Let's reread the story we started yesterday, called 'Tomorrow.' As we reread and as we read on, too, we know Toad has a problem. It isn't a spilled ice-cream cone; it is a messy house. But Toad has a choice, just like you do when your ice cream drops into the sand. How will he respond to his problem, to his trouble?

"We know that whatever he does will show us something about what he is like as a person, as a character." I reread the first two pages of Chapter 1.

Toad woke up.

"Drat!" he said.

"This house is a mess.

I have so much work to do."

Frog looked through the window.

"Toad, you are right,"

said Frog. "It is a mess."

Toad pulled the covers

over his head.

"I will do it tomorrow,"

said Toad.

"Today I will take life easy."

"What I do first is pause and think, 'How does the character *respond* to the trouble, the problem?' Hmm, what *does* Toad do?"

"I see you have an idea." I acknowledged students' raised hands, nodding. "Are you thinking that it seems like Toad tries to ignore the problem? He pulls the covers over his head." Reenacting Toad, I pulled imaginary covers over my head and, pretending to be Toad, said, "Go away, mess!" He doesn't want to even *look* at his messy house, right? He says he'll do it tomorrow. Is that what you were noticing, too?" The students were with me.

"So after I think, 'How does the character respond to the problem?' I think, 'What does that say about what kind of person he (or she) is? Hmm." I looked back at the book and paused. "It takes some thinking, doesn't it? His house is messy so he goes under the covers of his bed, saying, 'Go away, mess.' What kind of person responds to a messy house *that* way?

"Show me a thumbs up when you have some ideas ready." I gave the class a moment to think.

"I see many of you have ideas. If this were reading time, I'd write my ideas on a Post-it, wouldn't you? That way I wouldn't forget them. We don't have time to write just now, but will you think what you'd put on a Post-it? What kind of person do you think Toad seems to be?" I gave them a minute to think. "Pretend to write that on a pretend Post-it." I did the same.

GRADE 2: SERIES BOOK CLUBS

Ask partners to talk about their ideas and then share out their thinking with the class.

"So, readers, let's share our ideas. Read your pretend Post-it to your partner." As the room filled with talk, I listened.

"I heard many of you say you think Toad is lazy and irresponsible. He has work to do, but he doesn't get started cleaning. Instead, he stays in bed and says he'll do it tomorrow.

"Did you have different ideas about Toad?" I called on several children to share.

"I think Toad is careless because he let his house get really messy and now he doesn't even care about cleaning it up," one student explained.

"I think Toad is also very sleepy because he just wants to stay in bed," another offered.

"Wow! I can jot those ideas, too. Do you see how we can learn even more information about the characters when we look carefully at how they handle the problems that they face?"

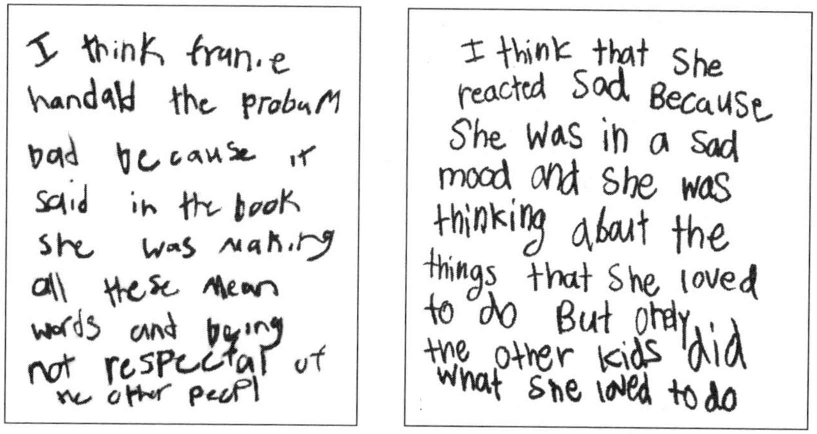

ACTIVE ENGAGEMENT

Channel the kids to notice the way another character responds to the same problem, letting them be the ones to go from noting what the character does to inferring what this means about his personality.

"In our Frog and Toad book, there is a problem—Toad's messy house—and, though this won't always be the case, in this story, we can see the way two different characters respond to that one problem. Will you and your partner peek into your book and see if your problem is the same way? Can you see if you have two different characters responding to the problem in your book?"

I gave children a minute to consider whether this was the case for their book as well. "Did you have two different characters perhaps responding differently to the problem?" After they had a moment to consider this, I pressed on.

"Let's think about this *same* story and, this time, let's think about how Frog responded to the problem of Toad's messy house. *And*, let's think what that shows about Frog as a character. Remember, the first thing to think about is, 'What does the character (Frog) do when there's a problem?'" I read on in the chapter:

Frog came into the house.
"Toad," said Frog,

FIG. 2–1 In these two jottings, both readers have an idea about the problem in the book. Rather than name the problem, they comment on the reaction and actions of the character to grow ideas.

FIG. 2–2 In these three jottings, the reader moves from a vague idea to a more concrete one and then jots about the main character's pattern of behavior.

SESSION 2: SERIES BOOK READERS PAY ATTENTION TO HOW CHARACTERS RESPOND TO PROBLEMS

> *"your pants and jacket
> are lying on the floor."
> "Tomorrow," said Toad
> from under the covers.
> "Your kitchen sink
> is filled with dirty dishes,"
> said Frog.*

"Now, turn and tell your partner, 'What does Frog *do* about the problem?'"

I listened in to collect responses before voicing back what I had heard. "So, we know that Frog isn't letting Toad just ignore the mess. He comes inside and points out all the things that need to be cleaned up.

"What do you need to think next?" Children called out that they needed to think, "What does this show about the kind of person Frog is?" and I agreed. "Turn and tell your partner the ideas you're having about the kind of person Frog is."

Again, I moved from partnership to partnership to listen in. "So, I heard you say a lot of things about Frog. Put your thumb on your knee if you agree with these things. I heard you say that Frog is responsible because he wants to fix the problem right away, and maybe he is a little bossy because he's telling Toad what to do." I noted that many kids agreed. "I know you had some other ideas about Frog, too. We can learn *so* much about the characters in our books by paying attention to what they do and how they handle problems."

By studying the character's actions and dialogue, you're nudging readers to draw conclusions about the character and describe his or her traits. You might find that children need more vocabulary to better articulate their ideas. Instead of supplying a trait, help children say, "He's the kind of person who always . . ." or "She's the kind of person who knows. . . ." Then, you might supply some words that describe these actions or characteristics. Say, "That's true. You know, a word for that is. . . . You might even say he/she is. . . ."

LINK

Set partners up to think about how the characters in their book respond to trouble and then to read on, collecting more information about the characters and their responses to problems.

"Readers, right now will you and your partner begin to think about how *your* character responds to trouble? I know you have marked the spot in your book where there is trouble. Remember to think first about what the character does, and then about what that might show about the kind of person the character is. And it may be that just like we did for Frog and Toad, you can study how different characters in your book respond differently to the same problem.

"Then, of course, you'll want to read on, collecting more information about your characters, more ideas about your characters, and noticing other problems that come up and the ways that the characters respond to those problems."

As students settled into their work, I sent some back to their reading spots and allowed others to continue working for a while in the meeting area.

By sending students off one by one to continue working at their independent reading spots, you'll allow yourself to concentrate your attention on students who may need additional support. You may choose to pull a small group of remaining students to offer more guided practice before transitioning them back to their spots.

CONFERRING AND SMALL-GROUP WORK

Thinking about Mood and Tone to Sound Like the Character

TODAY YOU MAY DECIDE to spend a bit of your time supporting that all-important skill of fluency. Second grade is the grade when children's fluency needs to surge. Remember that fluency involves phrasing, pacing, and prosody. Ultimately, for fluency to pay off and to strengthen comprehension (as it must), it becomes especially important for you to support prosody. One way to help children with prosody is to help them be aware of the mood or the tone of a scene to read in ways that reflect that mood or tone.

Identify children who read without expression and pull them together in a small group to work on reading fluently.

You may call together a small group of readers to help them with this strategy. Choose readers who tend to read in a monotone, expressionless voice. These children might read dialogue appropriately, but no matter who is talking or what that person is saying, the dialogue sounds the same.

When you call these children over you might say, "Now that you guys really know your character, you don't want to read each scene so it sounds as if *anyone* is talking; instead, you want to read it in a way that sounds like your character. To do this, you might go back and reread a scene really thinking who your character is talking to, how your character is feeling, and what the mood of that scene is."

"So right now, find a scene with lots of talking. Then, mark those pages with a Post-it." Help kids locate scenes with conversations between characters and prepare to coach readers to think about reading dialogue with clear, expressive voices and changing their intonation or tone to reflect each character.

(*continues*)

MID-WORKSHOP TEACHING
Paying Attention to Secondary Characters, Too

"Can I stop you for a moment? Your eyes are glued to your book just like I bet they are glued to the TV when you watch a favorite show! Quick! Tell me what sorts of problems your characters are facing and something that you have collected or observed about who they are as a person." I pointed at children around the room as they voiced out characters problems and what that said about them.

"Fox is trying to babysit, and the kids are misbehaving. He is frustrated and yells at them," one child reported back.

"Pinky is afraid that he won't win the spelling contest. He's acting really confident even though he is scared."

"Cam Jansen. She is trying to find stolen diamonds. She's not even scared. She's super smart, too!"

"Here's a tip. Readers don't just collect information and think about *one* character in their series books. They do the same thing with *other* characters as well. Just like we all did with Frog *and* Toad. Reread the page where you've marked things about *one* of your characters, and see if you can go back to learn about *another* character. What is *that* character like? How does he or she respond to the problem?"

SESSION 2: SERIES BOOK READERS PAY ATTENTION TO HOW CHARACTERS RESPOND TO PROBLEMS

As the kids mark the scenes in their books, coach in saying, "Are there lots of opportunities to practice reading dialogue on this page, or is only one character talking? Find a place where at least two different characters are talking back and forth."

As the kids begin to read, stop them and say, "So, who is your character talking to here? Think about how he might sound," or "Wait, read that line again using a different voice to see which one fits your character the best," or "What's the mood in this scene? Is the tone happy, is it sad, is it slow, is it fast? How might that impact the way that your character might sound? Think about how the other characters might sound as they respond to the main character."

The idea is that kids are using the information that they have gathered as they accumulate text to reread with the type of fluency that will ultimately aid the inference work required to deepen their comprehension of the series books they are reading.

After coaching into each reader a few times as they reread their scenes, stop the group before sending them back to their spots to say, "So remember, readers, it is important to reread some of the scenes in your books, to really make the scenes come to life. It is not that you just want to sound smooth or like a storyteller when you reread, but instead you want to make your characters pop off the page and come to life. To do this, you need to really think about your character and how he or she would sound given the circumstances of the scene."

SHARE

Talking Back and Forth about One Idea

Invite partners to share their thinking about their characters with each other, taking turns talking and listening. Remind them to refer to the text and to build on each other's ideas.

"Readers, it's time for our share session. Remember to bring your books, Post-its, and a pen to the meeting area and sit with your partner." I waited for children to settle in their spots.

"So, did you all learn *a lot* about your characters? From the way your books are marked up with lots of ideas, I can tell there are so many experts in this room! Remember, you learn about characters every step of the way in your books. You and your partner can share what you were thinking. Maybe you'll have similar ideas, or maybe you'll think differently.

"As you share, remember, one partner will go first. Partner 1, say your thought and reread the part that made you think it.

"Partner 2, you should open your book to that part, too. Listen to your partner. To be a good listener, remember to add on and/or ask questions about what your partner said *before* you put a new idea out there. *Then*, Partner 2, share if you had the same idea or a different thought about that same part of the story.

"After you have talked back and forth about one idea, then Partner 2 can share another idea and bring up a new part! Get started!"

FIG. 2–3 These partnerships are talking about their ideas and rereading parts out loud together to discuss their discoveries about characters.

Session 3

Series Book Readers Notice Similarities in Their Characters across a Series

IN THIS SESSION, you'll teach children that readers look closely for things that are similar in their series books by thinking about what the character always does or how the character usually feels.

GETTING READY

- Organize children into series book clubs by putting together groups of two partnerships reading books from the same series. Ask children to sit with their book club in the meeting area, where you have placed a sign with the name of the series (see Connection).
- Create a new book club chart titled "Book Clubs Talk Together." Display this chart if you made it in the last unit of study, so that it is ready to refer to (see Connection).
- Prepare to read the next chapter in your demonstration series book. We suggest "The Kite" in *Days with Frog and Toad* (see Teaching and Active Engagement).
- Display the anchor chart, "Series Readers Become Experts on Characters," so it is ready to refer to and be ready to add the strategy—"Notice the things that are the SAME across the series" (see Link).
- Make sure children bring their books, Post-its, and pens to the meeting area (see Share).
- Create a chart that outlines the three steps of sharing a discovery (see Share).

MINILESSON

CONNECTION

Announce that two sets of partners are reading in the same series, and that makes a club. Suggest that one set of partners swap books with the other partners, giving each other book introductions.

"Readers, do you remember that there aren't just two of you reading your series? There's another partnership that has been reading a *different* book in the same series. All the kids reading your series are members of a book club. You'll see that I have left signs on the rug to show you where each club should sit."

Remind children how they previously worked in goal clubs, and that series books clubs have some of the same rules and routines.

"Remember how you met in goal clubs in our last unit of study? Series book clubs are just the same, except now you can discuss your specific series." I reminded children to remember the rules we had established in the last unit of study, which I had written up as a new chart, as a tool for book clubs.

Book Clubs Talk Together
- *Look at the person talking.*
- *Nod or comment to show you are listening.*
- *Ask someone a question about what someone said.*
- *Give every voice a chance to speak.*
- *Let the speaker finish before you start talking.*

"Readers, when you finish the book you are reading, you'll have a chance to swap books with the other members of your club who have been reading another book in the same series. Some of you have already finished your book, and some of you need more time—when you finish not just reading but also rereading and talking about your book, then swap it."

Tell partners to tell each other one thing they learned about the star character of their series. Listen in and then announce that you have learned your teaching point from the class.

"Can you also tell your clubmates just a few sentences that tell *all about* the book? But, don't give away the *whole* story! Would you do that now even if you haven't quite finished the book you are reading?"

After children talked a bit, I voiced over saying, "I know you have been telling all about the book. Is there something you could tell your clubmates about the character who is the star of your series?"

The children talked and I listened. As they told each other what they'd discovered about the character, things emerged that are true across the books. Acting as if the fact that books in a series have similarities was just dawning on me, I stood up from listening to a few partnership and said to the whole class, "Whoa! This is interesting. Today, I'm learning my teaching point from you. See if I'm right."

❖ **Name the teaching point.**

"Today I want to teach you that when you read a bunch of books across a series, sometimes you'll notice things about the character that are *the same* in book after book!"

TEACHING AND ACTIVE ENGAGEMENT

Point out that readers of series books often find that the character is the same in in more than one book.

"Thumbs up if you and your club mates already found something about your character that seems similar in both the books!" Lots of kids so indicated. Gesturing to kids and to a series that I knew well, I confirmed what the kids said. "I found the same thing! Biscuit—he's always getting in trouble!

"Well, you're right! Series books are pretty predictable. Picking up a series book is a lot like tuning in to watch a new episode of your favorite TV program—the characters are often the same, and the things that they do are often the same. Cam Jansen is always—solving a crime, Mudge is always—drooling on Henry, and Biscuit is always—what?"

Christina piped in, "Getting into some sort of trouble," and I nodded.

Start reading another story in the whole-class series, channeling kids to join you in noticing ways the main character is the same across the two stories.

"Let's start a new story about Frog and Toad, remembering that when readers read a bunch of books across a series, they often notice things about the character that are the same in each book. Let's be on the lookout for things that

If you find, in your second-grade classroom, that you have a range of readers, you will want to mention, use, and show that range of texts throughout the unit. This way, all readers will not only feel a sense of value but will understand and see how the work applies to them. Maybe you have a group of series readers reading Biscuit. Maybe you have a group of readers reading Encyclopedia Brown. Whatever the case may be, you will want all readers to 'see themselves' reflected in this unit.

are the same in this next story. Partner 1, will you pay close attention to ways Frog is the same in this next story? And, Partner 2, will you pay close attention to ways Toad is the same? When you notice something that's the same (it might be something they do over and over, or ways of feeling that you see over and over), put your thumb on your knee. Let's work together to think, 'What do we notice about the character in this book that is the same as in the story we already read?'"

I turned to "The Kite" in *Days with Frog and Toad* and began to read the first four pages aloud. I paused after reading:

> *Toad ran back to Frog.*
>
> *"Frog," said Toad,*
>
> *"this kite will not fly.*
>
> *I give up."*

"Partner 2s, I see some of you with thumbs up. Are you noticing something that's the same?" The children nodded. "Turn and tell your partner." I leaned in to listen and then voiced back what I had heard. "I heard lots of you say that Toad is giving up. He has a problem and he's not trying to fix it, just like in the first story, 'Tomorrow.'

"Let's read on. Partner 1s, listen closely to study Frog." I read on:

> *"We must make a second try,"*
>
> *said Frog.*
>
> *"Wave the kite over your head.*
>
> *Perhaps that will make it fly."*

"Oh! Now I'm noticing Partner 1s signaling that they have ideas. Partner 1s, have you noticed something about Frog? Is he doing something that feels the *same* as the first story? Turn and tell your partner." I listened in, once again, and voiced back a few responses.

"I heard a few of you say that Frog isn't letting Toad give up, just like he didn't let Toad push off his house chores until tomorrow. Thumbs up if you agree! And some of you said that Frog is trying to fix the problem. Wowie! Isn't that the same as in the first story, too?"

I read on, stopping once more to consider emerging patterns. "It seems like Toad is feeling very frustrated. He was frustrated by all the chores in 'Tomorrow.' I wonder if Toad is *always* easily frustrated. But Frog feels very calm. It seems like Frog always feels calm and happy. We'll need to be on the lookout to discover if this is the same in book after book."

Set students up with a clear listening lens so they are better equipped to apply the strategy. In this lesson, you'll notice that I give each student in the partnership a different lens with which to study the text.

Notice how I voice back what I heard partners say inside their turn-and-talks rather than call on children to elicit responses. This helps me stay in control of the focus and pace of the lesson.

LINK

Tell students that when they start another book in a series, they can expect a lot to be the same, and suggest they mark these things with Post-its to discuss with their club later.

"Readers, it's time to go off and continue in your series! Many of you are starting new books in your series, ones that you swapped with other members in your club. Before you leave the meeting area, tell your club members just a couple more things about your book.

"As you start your new series book, you can expect that there will be *lots* that is the same. When you find those things, mark them with a Post-it. Then, in your club, the four of you can discuss the things that you are learning about your characters across the series: who they are, what they are like, and how they respond to problems and trouble. Together you can discover even more ways characters are the same in different books in the series. Let's add this strategy to the chart." I added the Post-it to the class anchor chart.

ANCHOR CHART

Series Readers Become
Experts on Characters

- Collect information about the main characters.
- Pay attention to how characters respond to problems.
- **Notice the things that are the SAME across the series.**

Notice the things that are the SAME across the series

SESSION 3: SERIES BOOK READERS NOTICE SIMILARITIES IN THEIR CHARACTERS ACROSS A SERIES   **19**

CONFERRING AND SMALL-GROUP WORK

Supporting Below-Benchmark Readers through Guided Reading

AS ALWAYS, you'll confer with individuals and partners and lead more than one small group during today's workshop. For your readers who are reading J or below, you are probably taking more frequent running records, so as to keep tabs on how they are problem solving words. You'll probably have some children who still need support being flexible and efficient in their word solving. Often you'll find readers who use the first part of a word and are not yet consistently reading all parts of the word, often neglecting the middle and end of the word. They may come up with a best-guess word based on the initial letters and not notice that the word doesn't work (doesn't make sense and/or doesn't look right).

These readers will benefit from a guided reading of the first book or two in a series. Let's imagine that a group of four is reading Fly Guy books, Level I. To plan your introduction, choose one book from the series. Make sure that you have enough copies of the book for everyone, and make sure to have read that book yourself, anticipating the places and even the specific words that will cause your readers to run into trouble. You'll want your introduction to support your students' work in a couple of those tricky parts, but you'll also want to leave a few parts for the children to work on during the guided reading session.

You might start the guided reading group with a two- or three-sentence preview of the series. For Fly Guy, you might say, "In each book in this series, there's a boy and a fly who have become friends, and they have little adventures." Then you can go on and talk a bit about the particular book in the series that the readers will be reading. Say a sentence or two about the main storyline. For those readers, you will not need to do a book walk. By second grade, your students are able to do this on their own, and you need to be helping readers with the specific skills you have decided to support—in this case, word solving, so that's where you'll invest the precious few minutes you have with these children during the book introduction.

You will want to bring children to one or two tricky parts and do a bit of word work. For example, you might point out a compound word and ask them to help you read the word in parts. On another page, you might have them locate a word and study the parts of that word. Then remind readers that there will be other tricky words they encounter and they need to use the same muscles with those words—looking across the whole word.

Your students should then be ready to read, and you'll watch, ready to give lean prompts such as, "Check the whole word," and "Read the next part."

MID-WORKSHOP TEACHING
Finding Differences, Too, in Characters across a Series

"Readers, I need to stop you. I see you all marking up many things that you are collecting that are the same about your characters! But when I talked to a few of you, some of you got a little worried because you found some things about your character that were actually *different*! I just want you to know that this will happen. As you look for things that are the same, you will ultimately also find differences!

"Right now, look over the last few parts that you have read in your book. Did you see differences? Any? If you did, that is another thing to notice and collect! You can bring those things to your club to talk about as well."

SHARE

Making Your Club Conversations Powerful

Suggest a way that club mates can talk about the similarities and differences they have spotted across the books in the series they are reading.

"Club time! Let's start our clubs by gathering in the meeting area. As always, bring your books, Post-its, and pens! It's time to share in your clubs. You'll share with your clubs in the same ways that you share with your partner.

"As you share, really listen to one another. If your club member says, 'I think that Frog is acting differently here than in the other stories' or 'I think Toad is being the same in this story as in the other story,' you, as club members, want to do *three* things." I counted the steps across my fingers: "One, show 'proof' or an example in the story; two, look in another book or story and decide if this is true there, too; and three, talk about it! Add on your thoughts and opinions and ask questions. It's like a little 'check' system! Then go on to the next idea!" I wrote these steps quickly on chart paper for book clubs to reference.

Series Book Club Readers Share Discoveries

1. Find proof in your book.
2. Look in another book or story to find at least one more example of your discovery.
3. Talk about it!

"Book club members, it's time to share our discoveries, not just about the characters in *one* of our books but across the series. Go ahead and start talking about your new favorite characters—who they are and the problems that they face."

FIG. 3–1 Book clubs cite evidence in the text to support their ideas.

Series Book Club Readers Share Discoveries

1. Find proof in your book.

2. Look in another book or story to find at least one more example of your discovery.

3. Talk about it!

I think...
Now I realize...

SESSION 3: SERIES BOOK READERS NOTICE SIMILARITIES IN THEIR CHARACTERS ACROSS A SERIES

Session 4

Series Book Readers Grow to Understand the Characters

IN THIS SESSION, you'll teach children that readers think about the things they have learned about the characters to understand them even better, like experts.

GETTING READY

- Prepare to read on in the demonstration text. We suggest using "The Kite" from *Days with Frog and Toad* (see Teaching and Active Engagement).
- Display the anchor chart "Series Readers Become Experts on Characters" and be ready to add the new strategy—"Think about what characters say and do"—to the chart (see Link).

MINILESSON

CONNECTION

Admire the way children have got to know their characters so well they now feel like friends. Then let your readers know this helps them think about their characters in new ways.

"Readers, does it feel like we're missing some people?" I looked over the heads of the class as if searching for someone and glanced at the classroom door. "Oh there you are!" I smiled and waved facetiously at an imaginary character standing in the doorway." Hi, Junie! Oh, that's right, I'm sorry. Junie *B.*! Come join us." I gestured for the kids to make space for Junie B. to sit with them. Then looking back up, I saw an imaginary Pinky standing at the edge of the meeting area, and waved him in as well. "And Pinky—glad you are here! Where's Rex? Henry! Does your Mom know you brought Mudge to school? He better not slobber on all our books! Wait, has anyone seen Cam? What do you think she might be off doing?

The kids called: "She's solving mysteries!"

"Maybe she'll solve the mystery of my lost glasses," I laughed and then turned to talk to the kids. "You've learned *so much* about the star characters in your series, that they don't just feel like characters anymore . . . they feel like friends! And here's the thing about someone you know as well as a friend. Being an expert and knowing a character *that well* means you can do some special *thinking* about them!"

❖ Name the teaching point.

"Today I want to teach you that when you are an expert on a character, you can understand that character like you understand your best friend. You can think, 'Why did he ___?' or 'Why did she ___?' and then you can think of answers, too."

22   GRADE 2: SERIES BOOK CLUBS

TEACHING

Help children think about how when you know a person or a character really well, you can understand them better.

"Have you ever been in a conversation with a whole group of kids and you look over at your best friend and you see that he's looking really upset, or really mad?

"And for a moment you think, 'Why is he mad?' But then, because this is *your* best friend, you can think back over everything and say, 'Oh, I bet I know what got him so upset.' *That's* what it means to be a best friend—you *get* the person. You can figure out *why* that friend does stuff. He gets up from the group and walks away, slamming the door, and everyone else says, 'What's with Billy?' And they shrug like, 'Who knows?' But you are Billy's best friend, so you think, 'I know.'

"Let's read on in 'The Kite' from *Days with Frog and Toad* and let's think about what we are learning about the characters, so we can understand them even better. We can ask *why* questions and then answer them, too." I turned to page 22, quickly recapping before reading on: "So we know that Frog and Toad are trying to fly a kite, but it won't get off the ground, and Toad just wants to give up. As I read, think about what the characters are doing and saying and feeling. Then, ask yourself, 'Why?' to help you understand them better."

> *Toad ran back to Frog.*
>
> *"This kite is a joke," he said.*
>
> *"It will never get off the ground."*
>
> *"We have to make*
> *a third try," said Frog.*
>
> *"Wave the kite over your head*
> *and jump up and down.*
>
> *Perhaps that will make it fly."*

"Let's stop here. I know that Frog is helpful. So, now I am going to think about him—and I'm going to ask that *why* question. Will you also push yourself to have a thought here? Hmm, I am wondering something. *Why* is Frog so patient with Toad? Hmm, maybe Frog isn't the type to give up easily. He tries and tries and tries, no matter what."

Then I added, "See how I asked 'Why?' and then when I wasn't sure, I pushed myself to use what I know about Frog to help me understand him better?"

Why did frankly frannie do the right thing insead of being lazy

Why did asuger told her tiscrat that's not nice and bosy.

Why didn't frank frannie act exited or so happy?

FIG. 4–1 By asking students to raise questions about the characters, you can assess their comprehension and help children prepare for club conversations. Here, "why" questions lead to richer conversations.

SESSION 4: SERIES BOOK READERS GROW TO UNDERSTAND THE CHARACTERS

ACTIVE ENGAGEMENT

Ask students to think about a character the way they would think about a friend. Point out that readers don't just learn stuff about the character, they also think about the character, asking *why* questions.

"Were you, too, thinking about Frog? Were you asking why? Were you wondering something? Quickly, turn and tell your partner what you were wondering about." I leaned in to listen to a few partnerships.

"Let me reread this passage again. Sometimes it helps to first name what you know about a character." I reread the same excerpt. Then, I invited kids to name out details they now knew about Toad.

Kids called out, one by one: "He gives up easily." "He's lazy." "He's feeling frustrated."

"Okay, now, push yourself to think even *more* about Toad! You can think about Toad, just like you would a friend, and ask yourself *why* he's feeling or acting the way he is. Then, grow ideas to answer your questions. Turn and talk."

After a few moments, I named some of what I'd overheard. "Readers, I hear so many interesting things that you are thinking about. Some of you were wondering, 'Why does he get so frustrated, so quickly?' Some others, over here," I pointed to a group of students in front left corner of the meeting area, "said that they thought Toad is super frustrated because it's like he is a two year old, and maybe Frog is like an older brother type. So many interesting questions and ideas!"

LINK

Send students off to discover, think, and wonder more about their characters, to understand them better across the series they are reading.

"So, readers, as you go off today to study the characters in your series, you are bound to learn even more about your characters. You will discover some of the same things that you already knew, as well as new things that you have never learned before.

"But remember, readers, as experts, you don't want to just *collect* information about your characters, you want to *think* about them and ponder and wonder. You'll especially want to ask *why* they do things! Being super curious not only helps you know even more about your characters but will help you understand more about who they are across the series." I added the strategy to the chart:

Think about what characters say and do

CONFERRING AND SMALL-GROUP WORK

Maintaining Students' Previous Work While Nudging Them to Do New Work

Continue to address students' assessment-based needs.

It's going to be important for you to keep in mind that while teaching this unit on series books, you are still really continuing the work of teaching your youngsters, and your focus will need to continue to be on supporting whatever assessment-based work your students need to do. Presumably you'll have students who still need to work toward more fluency, and you'll be helping those students read in phrases, scooping up more words at a time. You'll help them use conversational tones as they read, making that voice in their head as intelligible as possible. Meanwhile, you will probably have other students who need help progressing up the ladder of text difficulty. When kids are reading series books in small groups, this is a perfect time to help them with a series that is a wee bit challenging, giving the club members an introduction to that new series and perhaps even reading a bit of the first series book aloud to them.

Coach students to develop ideas that are not stated in the text and to use evidence from the text to support those ideas.

As you do all of that general instruction, you'll also want to keep in mind the work you've been teaching students to do lately. Although you didn't today teach students to compare and contrast, that instruction should be in the air in your classroom, so you'll absolutely want to watch to see whether students are continuing to initiate this way of thinking and if they are not, to nudge them to do so. When students do say, "The character is the same in these two books," make sure they extend that by saying, "Because, for example, on this page in this book . . . ," and then opening the text and reading from that passage. That is, you'll see that kids tend to make generalizations and they don't ground them in precise evidence from the text. Helping them to do that is important.

Today's instruction takes the work on this bend to a whole new level. Instead of asking students to report back on what their books have said, you'll now be asking them to develop ideas that probably are not in the text at all. Of course, when kids ask 'why' questions they also need to learn that they can muse over possible answers, entertaining responses to their questions. Teach them to think, "Perhaps it's because—" and "One reason he does this might be that—." As kids go to answer their own questions about the text, you'll want to encourage them to look in the texts for information that can ground their answers.

MID-WORKSHOP TEACHING
Finding Important Post-its to Think about More

"I'm hearing you ask really thoughtful 'why' questions: 'Why didn't Pinky just ask for help!?' 'Why does Michael act so mean?' 'Why doesn't the teacher tell them to stop?' Here is another great question: 'Does the little girl ever get mad at Biscuit?'

"Do you hear how your classmates are thinking about their characters? They aren't just *naming* what a character is like and how he or she acts, they are *thinking* about these facts. Look back over your Post-its now, and pick one that is thoughtful. And here's the challenge. Try to think even more about that one idea. Come up with more questions that go with your idea."

I let children do that for a minute and then I said, "When you read, you almost carry those questions with you. You think, 'What does the text say?' and keep reading. You might even stick your question to your arm so you can see it as you read on," and I stuck a Post-it to my sleeve to make my point. "Either way, you have twenty more minutes for reading."

SHARE

Readers Share Their Best Thinking to Make Book Clubs More Interesting

"I KNOW you are dying to talk with your club mates about your book. But, listen, it is beginning to feel like your clubs are real clubs. The only thing is: they don't have special names! How can you have a club that has no name? Here's one other worry I have. Your clubs don't have meeting spots. Doesn't your club need a special place to meet?

"So right now, will you get together with your club? But before you do anything else, decide if you need a name, and if so make one up. Decide if you need a clubhouse—a meeting spot—and if so, choose one and go to it. Just make sure you choose a place where you can do your best work."

After a bit, I said, "Club members, if you haven't yet decided on a name, do that later because I know you have books that deserve a conversation. *But*, don't just start talking about those books. Instead, think long and hard first. Think about this: What is the *best thinking* you have done about your series book?"

I gave kids space to think about that. "Hopefully your best thinking is on a Post-it. Star it. Then find another good thought (or make one) and star that too." After a minute, I said, "Now share your ideas—the ones that you think will make other people go, 'Hmm, that's interesting.'"

Kids talked for a bit. I voiced over, saying "Remember, listen carefully and add on to keep the talk going. To help you talk about your ideas for a *long* time, make sure you and your club members are giving proof and examples. Open up your books and look across the whole series to see if you can add on to what one another says. If you need to, use our chart from our last unit, 'Working Together in Goal Clubs.' These things will help you have a strong conversation as well."

FIG. 4–2 This reader looked over four Post-its to determine which ones were most important to talk about. Then he starred the ideas he thought were best to share with his club.

Session 5

Series Book Readers Use What They Know about the Characters to Predict

MINILESSON

CONNECTION

Relay a pretend scenario for the main character(s) of your demonstration text and ask children to predict what the characters might do next.

"Readers, imagine, for a moment, that you are in the world of Frog and Toad. Do you see those two friends and their homes and the woods in which they live? Now say that something unusual happens in their lives! A big hot air balloon comes to their forest—the kind with a basket attached that you can ride in. Do you know the kind I mean?

"Now say that Frog and Toad and all the other animals of the forest have been invited to go on a ride in this balloon—but here's the deal: they have to get up at the crack of dawn, before it's even light, and it's cold outside. It's late fall and the leaves have fallen off the trees. But if they go, they will have a once-in-a-lifetime opportunity to fly over the trees and water and land below, and to see a beautiful sunrise.

"How do you think Frog will react? What about Toad? Will they take that balloon ride? Turn and tell your partner!"

I gave children just thirty seconds to talk and then said, "How many of you guessed that Frog would jump at this opportunity, that he would try to convince Toad how fun it would be to take a balloon ride together? Thumbs up if you said something like that!" Lots of thumbs went up. "And how many of you thought that Toad might hesitate? Maybe he would say that going up in a balloon is dangerous or that he would rather stay under his warm covers and sleep in?" Again, lots of thumbs went up.

"I think you're right. Now that we know a lot about Frog and Toad, we can almost guess what they might do, even in a story that isn't written! And that's because you know the predictable ways in

IN THIS SESSION, you'll teach children that once they come to know the star character of a series well, they can draw on their knowledge of the character's behavior to almost predict that character's next steps.

GETTING READY

- Have a picture of a hot air balloon on hand if this is an unfamiliar concept for your students (see Connection).

- Display the anchor chart, "Series Readers Become Experts on Characters," and be prepared to add the strategy, "Use what they know to guess what the character will do next." (see Connection).

- Prepare to read another chapter in your demonstration text. Have a document camera or other means to display the text. We suggest the chapter, "The Hat" in *Days with Frog and Toad* (see Teaching).

- Make sure children have Post-its handy when they read so they can jot and mark ideas (see Mid-Workshop Teaching).

which each of these friends thinks and acts. You know that Frog is more optimistic and daring, and Toad is a creature of habit—he is less daring and more into comforts."

❖ **Name the teaching point.**

"Today I want to teach you that when readers know a character really well, the way you know your best friend or someone in your family, they can guess what that character will do next."

I added a new strategy to the anchor chart and had the children read it with me.

> **ANCHOR CHART**
>
> Series Readers Become Experts on Characters
>
> - Collect information about the main characters.
> - Pay attention to how characters respond to problems.
> - Notice the things that are the SAME across the series.
> - Think about what characters say and do.
> - **Use what they know to guess what the character will do next.**

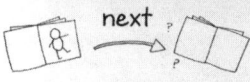

When imagining the world of Frog and Toad, you may want to have on hand a picture of a hot air balloon in case there are children in your class who don't know what one is or looks like.

TEACHING

Channel kids to join you in doing this work in the second story of the class series. Then, once the students are trying the work, show them how you'd do it.

"So let's try this now, in an actual Frog and Toad story, and will you watch how I use my knowledge of Toad to imagine what Toad might do next? You can try it with me. If you figure out something, too, just put your thumb on your knee, so I know you have a guess."

I opened up *Days with Frog and Toad* to the story "The Hat" and placed it under the document camera, and said, "Read this story with me and let's think about Toad and all the things we know about him and then let's guess what he will do next!"

I read the first page of "The Hat" and then said, "Oh, boy, I see some thumbs, some of you have some guesses about what Toad will do. Well, I know that Toad is a bit lazy and he acts kind of like a two-year-old and he really likes his friend Frog. I think he is going to just wear a hat that is just too big for him. Anyone think something different?"

Even during your demonstration, you'll want to ensure kids are actively listening. You might consider simple ways to engage students during your teaching by prompting them to think alongside you and give a silent gesture to signal they have an idea in mind. You'll notice in this lesson that a few children are invited to share out their predictions, but know that you need not elicit responses, especially if you're being mindful of pace. Students will have an opportunity to participate during the active engagement.

"I don't think he will," offered one student.

I responded, "Why? What about Toad do you know that you think he won't wear the hat?"

"I know that he gives up. So I think he will give up the hat and be like, 'No, no, the hat is too big, I can't, I can't!'"

"Two *different* thoughts, but both have really good reasons! Let's see!" I read on to page 43.

"Toad really is too ridiculous and silly! He's going to wear that hat! Well, did you see, though, what we did? Because we know Toad so well, we made a good guess about what might happen. Remember, sometimes you will be right and sometimes you won't be, but as a series book reader, it is fun to try!"

ACTIVE ENGAGEMENT

Continue reading together with children, asking them to make predictions with their partners by using all that they know about the characters.

"Let's read on together and see if we can guess what Frog will do!" The class continued to read together. I stopped after page 46, when Toad was fast asleep, dreaming and having "big thoughts." "We know a lot about Frog, don't we! Tell your partner a bunch of things that you know about Frog." I gave partners a few moments to share their thoughts with one another, while I listened in.

"So, I heard you say that Frog is helpful, he is patient, and he knows the right answer a lot of the time. He isn't as silly as Toad. Using what you know about Frog, what is he likely to do? Take a guess and whisper it to your partner!"

"Readers, when you are predicting what might happen next in a story, you don't actually know for sure *what* will happen. So readers often think, 'Maybe the story will go like this, or maybe it will go like that.' I heard you suggesting some 'maybe' predictions to each other.

"Some of you are predicting that Frog might buy Toad a new present. And those you of who predict that have reasons for that prediction. You point out that Toad is nice that way. I heard one of you suggest that Frog might buy Toad not just any ol' present but a new hat—one that fits. Again, you had reasons to back up that prediction. Frog is thoughtful *and* he knows the problem Toad is having with the hat. I heard some others suggest that Frog might try to teach Toad some sort of lesson—and you are right, in stories like this, characters often learn lessons. *All* of these seem like good predictions—and I love that you have reasons to support your predictions.

"Should we read on a bit to see which we think might happen?" The kids chimed yes, and we read pages 47–49 together, as a shared reading.

You'll want to encourage students to ground their predictions by supplying reasons or details from the text. Nudge readers to consider multiple possibilities, thinking "Maybe . . . or, "maybe instead . . .".

At that point, I lowered the book and said, "Oh, wow! None of us quite guessed that, but *all* of us knew that Frog was going to help fix the problem! Good guessing work, second graders!"

LINK

Move students to transfer the work of using what they know about characters to guess the characters' next steps into their own series books.

"So, today, when you get back into your series, remember, don't just collect stuff that you know about your series or about the star of your series. Instead, you will want to do as we have been doing. You will want to use what you know about characters to be able to ask big questions—like 'why' questions—and to understand your character the way you understand your best friend. *And* you want to use what you know to predict, to guess, what the character will probably do next. Then as you read on, you can think, 'Yep! I knew it.'

"Try it right now. Look over what you read yesterday. Reread a bit of yesterday's part." I gave them a minute to do this. "Now, think—can you make a little guess about what might happen next? Think about what you already know about your character and think, 'What would this character do next?' When you have an idea, put your thumb on your knee."

I listened to a few, one-to-one, and then I said to the rest of the class, "If you have a guess, read on. If you don't, keep rereading and thinking, 'What do I know about my character? What do I think that my character will do next?' Everyone, off you go to your reading spots!"

During today's link, you'll offer your students another opportunity to practice the strategy, but this time in their own books. By doing so, you're not only giving students ample support with applying the strategy, but you're also implicitly communicating that this is a strategy they can use in all of their books, not just to predict what may happen next in Frog and Toad.

CONFERRING AND SMALL-GROUP WORK

Lifting the Level of Your Students' Predictions

IF YOU DECIDE that today you'd like to use the workshop as a time to lift the level of your students' predictions, you might distribute a very large colored Post-it to each student and, at some point, use a voiceover to ask all students to pause and think, "What might happen next? Record a prediction." Then you could convene a small group of readers to bring attention to the kinds of information that readers use to make predictions not just before they read but as they read. Use this list as a rubric to assess where students fall and then nudge them to make more and more informed predictions. For example, if most are simply predicting the final action in the book, you might suggest that's level 1 work. Then level 2 could be for students who read, pausing from time to time to predict what will happen next. Perhaps level 3 is for students who draw on details from the text to make those predictions, and level 4 could be those who also draw on knowledge about how stories tend to go.

Students could self-assess their own predictions, laying them alongside some you may have made to go with the class read-aloud. Then they could work in pairs to lift the level of their predictions. A student who had predicted what would happen but not how, could revise to include the how. A student who had predicted the actions characters will take but not the details, could provide some details to support the prediction. A student who had predicted the characters' actions and provided details might be encouraged to add in a common story element. For example, a reader might know that the main character usually encounters a problem toward the beginning of a story, and then use this knowledge to make a better prediction.

MID-WORKSHOP TEACHING **Jotting Ideas and Surprises**

"Readers, when you stop and predict what the character might do next, it's important that as you read on you check your prediction. Most of the time, you'll find you were right! The character did exactly what you knew he would. You might jot a few words on a Post-it about these things that keep happening and stick that Post-it on a page that shows an example.

"But sometimes the character may surprise you! Those are my favorite parts of a story. You'll want to stop at those parts and ask that question you learned the other day: Why? Why did the character do that or say that or react that way? If there are places where the character's motivations seem especially puzzling to you, when you really don't understand why he or she did something—leave that *Why?* on the page and then you can talk about it later with your club."

SHARE

Growing Ideas in Book Clubs

Push students to grow ideas by asking questions and using what they know about the series to discuss possible explanations.

"Readers, will you gather all your materials and join your club at your special meeting spot?" I gave the students a moment to settle into their spots around the classroom. "So, right now, find a place in your book that surprised you or made you wonder. It might be a place where the character acted, or reacted, in a certain way that gave you lots to think about. I bet you can't wait to discuss with your club! Decide who will begin your book talk. Then, remember to listen closely and add on to keep the ideas growing and the conversation going. Get started!"

I moved in to listen in to one club, coaching partners to respond and clarify to support a building discussion. "Sometimes talking about the questions you have can help you understand characters better. You might say, 'I don't understand why . . .' Then, you can discuss possibilities with your clubmates. Push yourself to say, 'Maybe it's because . . .,' to grow ideas that explain the character's actions or reactions to events in the story."

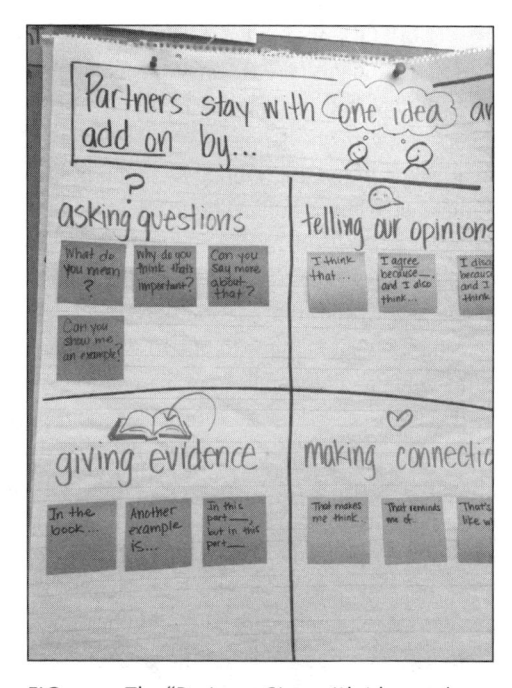

FIG. 5–1 The "Partners Stay with Idea and Add On" chart is an example of a chart that supports partnerships and book clubs in sharing and extending their ideas.

Session 6

Series Book Readers Learn about Characters from Their Relationships with Other Characters

IN THIS SESSION, you'll teach children that readers get to know the different people in a character's life and compare them to their own relationships so that they to get to know and understand their character even better.

MINILESSON

CONNECTION

Suggest that to get to know someone, it's best to watch that person relating to others—lots of others. This is also true for researching characters.

"Did you know that there are adult researchers who study kids? Like, a researcher could knock on this door and say, 'Could I come in? I'm doing research on so and so, and I'd like to observe him.' Here is my question. If a researcher wanted to watch you and learn about what you are like as a person, do you think we should put a desk at the back of the room, away from everyone, facing the wall, and have you work at that desk for the next few weeks so the researcher could really watch you? *Or* do you think that to get to know you, it would be best for the researcher to watch you in your book club, and when you are talking with a partner?"

The kids chimed in that the researcher would need to watch them while in book clubs and other projects.

"So, for you to have really deep thoughtful ideas about your characters—whether we are talking about Julian, Amber, Junie B., or even Toad, you are saying that *you* (you are the researcher, now) need to pay close attention to the relationships the characters have. You can't just think about how they are when they are alone—you need to think about how they are with other people."

GETTING READY

- Display the anchor chart, "Series Readers Become Experts on Characters," and be prepared to add the new strategy, "Notice what a character's relationships show" (see Connection).

- Prepare to show a text, in which the main character(s) have relationships with other characters, to talk about those relationships and what readers can learn about their character from them. If possible, project the text under the document camera. We suggest *Pinky and Rex and the Bully* (see Teaching).

- Use another familiar text, in which the main character(s) have relationships with other characters, to talk about those relationships and what readers can learn about their character from them. We suggest using the text from shared reading, *The Stories Julian Tells* (see Teaching).

- Make sure students bring their series books and Post-its with them to the meeting area (see Active Engagement and Link).

- Display the anchor chart, "Keeping Track of Longer Books," from the previous unit and provide individual copies for students (see Mid-Workshop Teaching).

33

"One more thing. If the researcher watches you with one person—say, the researcher watches you with the principal—-will he know all about how you act with all people? Or does the researcher have to watch you with different people—like with the principal *and* with your friends?"

The children, of course, were quick to recognize that they are different in different relationships. I added the new strategy to the anchor chart.

ANCHOR CHART

Series Readers Become Experts on Characters

- Collect information about the main characters.
- Pay attention to how characters respond to problems.
- Notice the things that are the SAME across the series.
- Think about what characters say and do.
- Use what they know to guess what the character will do next.
- **Notice what a character's relationships show.**

Notice what a character's relationships show

✤ Name the teaching point.

"Today I want to teach you that to have deep ideas about a character it helps to study that person's relationship with others. What's the person like when in one relationship? Another? How does the character act around other characters?"

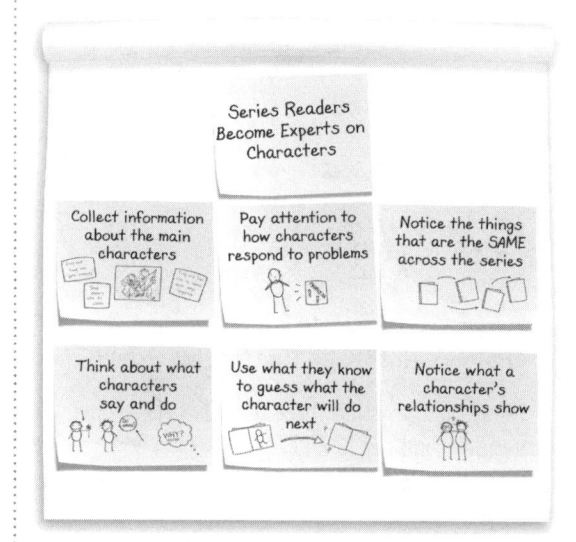

34 GRADE 2: SERIES BOOK CLUBS

TEACHING

Review your point—that you can learn about a character by how he or she interacts with different characters—by talking about a character's many sides.

"So, let's think about some of the relationships the characters in our books have. Then, we can think, 'How is this helping me get to know the main character even better?' Let's practice with a few books we know well."

I placed *Pinky and Rex and the Bully* under the document camera. "In this book, we know more about Pinky because of his relationships. We know about his relationship with his friend Rex, but do we then say, 'Okay! Now I know all there is to know about Pinky!' No way!

"Because we *also* get to know Pinky by seeing what he is like with Kevin, the bully. Those of you who are friends with Pinky, think for a minute about whether Pinky is the same when he is with Rex and when he is with that bully." The children all started saying, "No way," and we soon established that with the bully, he's shy, maybe even afraid.

You'll want to draw upon past read-aloud texts and use characters and relationships that are familiar to your students. If needed, replace this example, using Pinky and Rex and the Bully, *with a class favorite.*

Recruit the class to join you in rereading a familiar book, this time noting the way a character's many sides come out when studying that character's different relationships.

I took out our shared reading text, *The Stories Julian Tells,* and placed it under the document camera. "This time, we're the researchers, watching a person to see what that person is like. Let's watch Julian when he is with his little brother, Huey, because that should show us a bit about Julian." I began rereading a bit of the story, "The Pudding Like a Night on the Sea," which I enlarged under the document camera.

Scanning through the pages, I murmured, "You gotta get to a part that acts like a window, letting you peep in on the person, like right . . ." I paused at page 7. "Let's reread this part, where Huey and Julian begin to eat the pudding." Looking back up at the class, I added a tip to help students transfer the learning to their own books. "Did you notice that I didn't start rereading at the beginning? Instead, I scanned through the text to find a part when Julian and Huey are doing something that I thought would be good to research."

"The Pudding Like a Night on the Sea" is introduced in Session 1 of the Read-Aloud. If you haven't done this lesson yet, consider taking time to do it now to lay a foundation of knowledge, before you and your students focus on the characters' relationships.

I began to read page 7. Pausing at the bottom of the page, I said, "Hmm, what are you thinking?" I added, "I do that. I just read a little, and then I pause and push myself to start having a thought already. So far, um, I'm thinking that they get along pretty well. Sometimes, Julian acts older. *But* sometimes he doesn't. Like here, in this part, when the two of

Note that my thinking follows the journey that I anticipate most children's thinking will follow. My first thought is pretty obvious. It's as I say more and think more that I come to something interesting.

them are eating up the pudding together, they are both acting—what would you say, mischievous? Julian is being the opposite of a responsible older brother, isn't he? Instead, it's like he and little Huey are partners in crime. Do you agree?" The students nodded.

ACTIVE ENGAGEMENT

Ask students to try out the work of studying a character's relationships to form new thoughts and learn more about the character.

"Can you do this work with the dad?" I asked. "What's the first step?"

The children pointed out that we had to skim to find a part that showed Julian and his dad, which I essentially did for them, settling on a part on page 12, when Julian's father is mad at the boys about eating all the pudding.

Giving children some direction, I turned to the page and said, "Now what?" until the children called out that we should reread that part. I nodded but pressed on. "And what are we thinking about as we reread?" Soon we were rereading, thinking about the relationship Julian and his dad have and what this shows about Julian.

I finished the page and then channeled the kids to talk in partners. I listened in as they talked, and then said, "Many of you are saying that Julian is very respectful of his dad. Julian knows when he has done something wrong."

Urge children to not only research the obvious signs of a character's relationship but also to think hard about that relationship. Are there good and bad sides to it? How is it like and unlike relationships other characters have?

"When you research character relationships, you can do your own thinking. I have some hard questions for you. First, is Julian's relationship with his dad all good, or is there something less than perfect about it? And next, how is it like, or unlike, the relationship other characters you know have with their parents? Turn and talk."

The room was electric as children talked about those two complicated questions. Soon the class took the questions up, agreeing that Julian pretty much said nothing back to his father, and maybe he should have done so. And no, he is nothing like Junie B. Jones! That would be an interesting friendship.

I debriefed, saying, "Do you see how thinking about the relationships in a book helps you know and say even more about your characters? It can really help you push your thinking about them! Different relationships will show you different things, often, about your characters!"

LINK

Channel students to apply what they've just learned to their own books, poring over an important interaction between characters.

"Now, it's your turn! Will you first turn to a part of your book where the characters are interacting in an important way?" I gave the children a minute to locate such a part, and then, whether or not they were all settled on a page, I pressed on. "Reread that part closely to *think* about the relationship the two characters have. Think, 'What do I know about this relationship, and how is the main character acting or feeling? What do I now know about my character because of this relationship?' As you reread and think, if you have time, jot your ideas on a Post-it. Do this now."

After a bit, I said, "Will you work now with your club? Talk about the different relationships that your character has and what you know about your character because of those relationships. Turn and talk." I floated around the meeting area, listening into the various things that the club said. I whispered into one club, saying, "So, do you know parts in your book that show that?" I gestured for them to reread. To another club I said, "*Why* is he feeling that way?" I prompted, "How was he acting around her earlier in the book? What has changed?" To a third club, I said, "What is this teaching you about the character?"

As you send children off to read, remind them once that among a lot of other things, they can study characters' relationships.

"Okay, series experts, are you ready to push yourself even more to think about your characters? Great! Remember, to learn even more, it's important to pay attention to not just the *main* character but also to the relationships that the main character has with other characters. Stop at parts where you can study the main character's relationship. Pay attention to what the character does and says. Then think, 'What am I learning about this relationship?' Be sure to jot your ideas on a Post-it to hold on to them. Ready, readers? Get started!"

Prompt students to talk with clubs, rather than just a partner. In this way, you'll be able to support readers as they apply strategies, as well as coach clubs to engage in book talk following agreed-upon rules for speaking and listening.

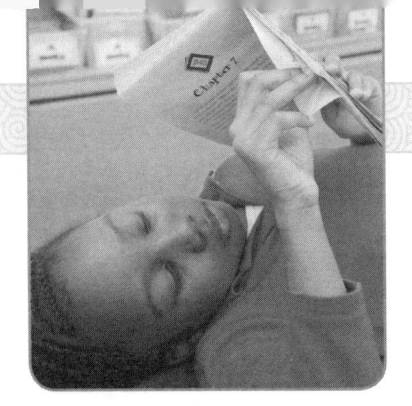

CONFERRING AND SMALL-GROUP WORK

Building Students' Skills in Reading Chapter Books

AS YOU CONFER and pull some strategy groups, you may decide to look for some typical things that second graders have difficulty with as beginning readers of chapter books. First, some of your readers may develop the habit of "word calling."

These readers may say all the words accurately, yet not really think about what is happening, pause on parts that are confusing, or recognize that they are encountering a new word. As your students are reading, you might check in every now and again and say, "So, what does that mean?" or "Is that confusing? Do you get what is happening here?" Some of your students may say no. Others may be able to explain. You may want to say to your reader, "As you are reading, make sure you pause and check in with yourself to be sure you understand what is happening. Oftentimes when I read, I need to reread parts to make sure I really get it."

Practice with your students and coach in to pause and have them check for meaning. Then watch and observe, how they check themselves.

Make sure students hold on to information across a whole chapter book.

Another common problem that some beginning chapter book readers have is linking the different parts and chapters together. Sometimes you will have readers who read each section as a stand-alone story. Say to your readers, "Remember, this whole book is one story, whether it takes place in one day or in one week. Before you start your next chapter you will want to remember the most important things that happened in the chapter before. Then ask yourself, 'Where, now, will the characters go and what will they do?' You want to make sure that it makes sense with what has already happened. Let's try that in your books. If you need to do a little rereading, start that now."

Then you will want to lean in and coach readers to link the various parts of their story together and to read on thinking about how this new part fits with the rest of the story.

Coach students to make Post-its only when they have important thoughts, not every time they have a thought.

Certainly, you will find that some of your students are 'over-Post-it-ers'—that is to say, their books have *way* too many Post-its. Instead of taking away all the Post-its, celebrate with your students that they are trying to generate *a lot* of thinking.

MID-WORKSHOP TEACHING
Monitoring Students' Understanding across Longer Books

"Readers, I want to stop you. I just saw Roman pull out this chart from our last unit and I want to congratulate him. It is so smart to draw on all that you have ever learned, and charts can remind you of those things." I held up the "Keeping Track of Longer Books" chart from the previous unit.

ANCHOR CHART

Keeping Track of Longer Books

- Ask your same book partner for help.
- Determine what's important.
- When you get off track, stop, reread, and answer questions.
- Write notes to help you keep track.

"So right now, I'm giving each one of you a copy of this chart. Will you read it over and star the bullets on this chart that continue to be important for you to do? Then get back to work, remembering that the chart can act like your own private teacher whispering tips to you. Keep the chart close."

Congratulate them and say, "This is exactly what you want to be doing in your head, thinking, *all* the time. And here's a tip to help you do this work even better. You don't need to write a Post-it *every* time you have a thought. Instead, only write down your most important thoughts, the ones you need to talk about with your partners and club members. Maybe you've marked a part that's confusing or a part where something really dramatic happens or a big change occurs. Let's look over the Post-its you made in the first part of your book. Look over them and say to yourself, which are the most important ones and why are they important? Are they helping you get ready to talk to your book club?"

Then coach students as they try this in a few parts of their books. You might say, "After you read a section or chapter, look over what you marked and ask yourself, what do I need to talk about with my partners and club? Only keep the most important ones."

SHARE

Keeping the Character Conversations Going

"READERS, it's club time! As you get into your clubs and begin to share the various things that you are learning and thinking about the characters, their problems, and their relationships, remember to not only *tell* your examples and proofs but actually *read* those examples out loud. Club members, if you have the same book, turn to the same part and read along. *Everyone* in the club, as you are listening, use the questions that you have been asking yourself as a reader in your conversations to help say *a lot* about that one moment in the book.

"You might also ask one another, '*Why* is he feeling that way?' or 'How was he acting around her earlier in the book? What has changed?' or 'What is this teaching you about the character or the relationship?' Anyone in the club can ask these kinds of questions and can also answer these questions to help each other dig deeper into the series. Remember, your club is like a team—work together!"

Keep the Character Conversations Going...

- Why is the character feeling that way?
- How was he/she acting earlier in the book?
- What has changed?
- What is this teaching you about the character or the relationship?

ns on Author's Craft   BEND II

Session 7

Authors Paint Pictures with Words

IN THIS SESSION, you'll invite children to join you in a class inquiry. Together, you will explore this question: "What do authors do to paint a vivid picture with words?"

GETTING READY

- ✓ Place on the easel a picture of a painting with a lot of detail that children can notice and describe. We use Georges Seurat's *A Sunday Afternoon on the Island of La Grande Jatte* (see Connection).
- ✓ Seat children in their clubs within the meeting area (see Teaching and Active Engagement).
- ✓ Display the first few pages of a series book using a document camera or other device. We use *Magic Tree House: Polar Bears Past Bedtime* (see Teaching and Active Engagement).
- ✓ Make a one-day chart, "How Do Authors Paint Pictures with Words?" to document the discoveries children make in their inquiry (see Teaching and Active Engagement and Share).

MINILESSON

CONNECTION

Invite children to study a painting, noticing and naming details about the subjects, their feelings and actions, and the setting.

"I've brought one of my favorite paintings with me today and I thought we could spend a few minutes studying it. It's called *A Sunday Afternoon on the Island of La Grande Jatte*. And it was painted by a famous painter named Georges Seurat. He worked incredibly hard to make this picture especially detailed. Would you believe Seurat painted this scene entirely with tiny dots and small brushstrokes? Let's notice all we can about this painting."

I placed the poster on the easel. "Look closely. What do you notice? Who's in this scene? Where is this taking place? What are the people doing? How do you think they're feeling? Give me a thumbs up when you have a few ideas ready." After a moment, I invited several children to share.

"They're all at a park near the water and there's lots of trees," Preston said, pointing to the details in the painting.

"Yeah, and it's really busy. There's lots of people walking around," Ella added.

"I think they're having a picnic. Look at the dogs playing," another child called out.

"It's sunny but they have umbrellas," a perplexed voice chimed in.

"You're right, there isn't any rain," I noted. "Why do you think these ladies have umbrellas?"

"It's because it's so bright and sunny. The umbrellas are blocking the sun, like at the beach," Sophia explained to the group. "It looks old-fashioned, too. Look at all of their clothes."

Point out the connection between artists and writers. Then tell children that as series book experts, they are ready to study what authors do to paint a vivid picture for readers.

We discussed the painting a bit more, paying attention to the details of the setting, the actions depicted across the painting, and the feelings of the different people. Then, I connected this careful observation work to the close reading readers do to envision the scenes in their stories.

"Are you wondering, 'Why are we studying this painting during reading workshop?' Yeah? Here's why! Your books are a lot like paintings and the authors are a lot like painters. But instead of using a paintbrush, authors use words.

"You're growing to be such experts on your series books, learning all that you can about the characters and what's happening in each story. Now, as series experts, you're ready for even *bigger* work. You see, expert readers know how important it is to pay attention not just to what the *character* is doing *in the story*, but also to what the *author* is doing *on the page*—the author's craft. So, instead of me telling you all the things authors do on the page to help paint that vivid picture for readers, let's work together to investigate some possible answers. Are you ready?"

Name the inquiry question.

"The question we will be investigating together is: 'What do authors do to paint a vivid picture with words?'"

TEACHING AND ACTIVE ENGAGEMENT

Invite children to read the first few pages of a book with you, and then work with club mates to name what the author did to paint a picture with words.

"Let's read the first few pages of *Magic Tree House: Polar Bears Past Bedtime*. And as we read, be sure to pay attention not just to what the character is doing but also to what the author is doing. Think, 'What parts really paint a vivid picture in my mind?' Then, we can name what the author is doing to paint that picture."

I opened up to the first page, masking the illustration, and invited the children to read along with me:

FIG. 7–1 *A Sunday Afternoon on the Island of La Grande Jatte* by Georges Seurat

You'll notice that we use Georges Seurat's painting A Sunday Afternoon on the Island of La Grande Jatte *because it is not only a beautiful piece of artwork but it also has so much detail for children (and adults alike) to study closely. You may choose to swap this painting for one of your own favorites.*

Whoo. *The strange sound came from outside the open window.*

Jack opened his eyes in the dark.

The sound came again. Whoo.

Jack sat up and turned on his light. He put on his glasses. Then he grabbed the flashlight from his table and shone it out the window.

A white snowy owl was sitting on a tree branch.

"Whoo," the owl said again. Its large . . .

I paused at the end of the first page and nudged children to think about the ways the author created a vivid scene. "Can you picture it? So can I! How did Mary Pope Osborne do that? Let's read on keeping with that question in mind." I turned the page and read the second page aloud:

[Its large] yellow eyes looked right into Jack's.

What does he want? Jack wondered. *Is he a sign, like the rabbit and the gazelle?*

A long-legged rabbit and a gazelle had led Jack and Annie to the magic tree house for their last two adventures.

"Whoo."

"Wait a second," Jack said to the owl. "I'll

This session builds on the work of Bend I and also on work children did in the final bend of Second-Grade Reading Growth Spurt, *in which they studied the craft moves of authors, thinking about authors' intentions. Those of you who follow the writing units of study will recognize that this work also mirrors the craft study that is at the heart of the Grade 2 writing unit,* Lessons from the Masters. *There are good reasons to return to a craft study again and again. First, this is sophisticated work. It requires children to look closely, to think analytically, to step back from the stance of reading a story to think about what went into the making of the story. This isn't easy. Practice is essential. Second, a study of craft merits repeat. All of us—whether we are eight years old studying* Owl Moon *or adults studying* Anna Karenina—*have the ability to see more in the construction of texts each time we step back to examine what authors do to pull it all together—from creating characters and setting, to plotting the events. There's much to admire and learn from.*

get Annie."

Jack's sister, Annie, always seemed to know what birds and animals were saying.

Jack jumped out of bed and hurried to Annie's room. She was sound asleep.

Jack shook her and she stirred.

"What?" she said.

"Come to my room," whispered Jack. "I think Morgan's sent another sign."

In a split second, Annie was out of bed.

"Thumbs up if that picture is getting even more vivid!" The kids signaled back. "Let's think about these first two pages. What parts really stand out to you? How did the author paint a picture?" I placed the first page under the document camera. "Look across the first page. What are some ways Mary Pope Osborne painted a picture with words here? Will you turn and share with your club?" As kids talked in small groups, I moved around the meeting area to listen in. After a minute or so, I called the group back.

Share out children's thinking and begin a chart, "How Do Authors Paint Pictures with Words?"

"I'm hearing lots of ideas! Let's start a list." I clipped a piece of chart paper on which I had written the title, "How Do Authors Paint Pictures with Words?" to the easel. "Maybe the Cam Jansen club can start us off. What did your group notice?"

"Well, in the beginning there was a sound word, so you could hear the owl," James noted.

"And it said that it was dark and that the sound was outside the window, so you could understand where it is," Dean added.

"Precisely! The author describes the setting. And includes sounds to help you not only *see* what's happening, but also *hear* it, too. Let's add that," I wrote the new details on the chart.

This minilesson teaches through inquiry. You'll set students up to study author's craft together. If you find your students are having a hard time finding things to name, you can do a couple of things to support them. One, you can give them examples of what other students say. Then give your students another opportunity with the same portion of the text (or a different part) to find and name things. The second thing you can do is give a quick demonstration and then give your students an opportunity to try again. In an inquiry, you want the class to work together to explore possibilities around a challenging question.

How Do Authors Paint Pictures with Words?
- Describe the setting
- Include sound words

"What else?" I called on another club to add to the list.

"You could see all the things Jack was doing, like getting the flashlight and shining it at the owl and then going to Annie's room to wake her up," Olivia named back.

I pointed to the lines of action across the first two pages. "That's true. When the author includes lots of actions, it helps you *see* what's happening. You do that in your writing, too. You use small actions to paint a picture in your stories. As I add that to our list, push yourself to think about how else the author paints a picture to help you really see what's happening in the story."

"You know what Jack is thinking because it says, '*What does he want?*' and then he whispered, '*Come to my room,*' to Annie," one student added.

Add more of the children's observations to the chart.

I echoed the student's response in a more transferable way. "You're right. The author includes lots of dialogue to help us know what characters are thinking and saying. That also helps us know how they might be feeling. And *whispered* even shows us *how* Jack is saying it. That makes the picture clearer in our minds, too." I added the observation to the end of the running list.

LINK

Remind children to keep in mind this list of ways authors paint pictures with words as they read.

"What an impressive list! You see, as you grow to become experts on the series books you read, you'll also grow to become experts on the authors of those books and the craft moves they make in those books. As you read, and reread, be sure to pay extra attention to all these ways authors paint a picture with words! Then, use them to make the picture in your mind extra vivid. That will help you understand the story, the characters, and the series even better."

CONFERRING AND SMALL-GROUP WORK

Supporting Attentiveness to Craft

Hold quick conferences to nudge students into the habit of really studying what the author does and why.

You'll probably hold a lot of quick conferences at the start of today's reading time. You may want to ask students, "What part did you find that painted a really vivid picture?" After the reader directs you to a particular passage, you might say to the whole tableful of readers, "Hey, Mario and I just found a part that really paints a vivid picture! You can practically *see* everything that's happening. Did you find one yet?" You could press on, saying, "We reread, asking ourselves, 'What do I see as I read this?' and then we marked it with a Post-it. When you find a part, mark it! And then figure out, 'How did the author do it? How did the author paint a picture with words?' Then look for a new part!"

You will want to help students explain what they notice about the craft moves an author has used. You may want to do a few voiceovers to the whole class about things that students are finding. For example, you might say things like, "Karina just saw that her author uses dialogue to show what characters are like. She makes the characters say things in funny ways, like they are talking in baby talk. The author could've just said, 'The little girl spoke in a babyish way.' *Instead*, when you read it, it actually sounds like a baby! Wendy just found, in her book, that her author does lots of the *same* things that Mary Pope Osborne does! Keep reading and discover more vivid parts everyone!"

Pull a group of below-benchmark readers to support their ongoing progress.

While supporting a new attentiveness to craft, you will want to make sure that you are also continuing to support your readers' progress as they move up levels of text complexity. You may decide to pull a group of readers who are below benchmark to help them revisit familiar books, this time having students pay attention not only to what happened but also to the accessible inference work.

You can say, "Once you have found a part in your book to research, you will want to stop and really study not just *what* is happening but also *why* it is happening. You can use a couple of things to help you: you can think about how the character is feeling and why, you can think about what the character is saying or how the character is behaving." You will want to refer back to the class chart, "How Do Authors Paint Pictures with Words?" Then, coach kids to think about how the author has helped them identify those feelings and think about how characters are acting.

MID-WORKSHOP TEACHING
Rereading When You Find Author's Craft

"Readers, guess what? I think almost every one of you has found a place in your book where the author has painted a really vivid picture with words, helping you see what's happening, where the scene is taking place, what the characters are doing and saying, and even how they are feeling. I want to urge you to spend a bunch of time just *rereading* that one part over and over, noticing more and more as you reread it. You might frame it with Post-its like Gabriella has done." I showed the children how Gabriella had torn Post-its into strips to edge the passage she was studying.

"The most important thing, though, is that you reread the passage. Reread it into your conch shell. (You remember how to read into that shell, right?) Reread it with feeling. Reread and make that picture in your mind even clearer. Then, close your eyes and really see it." I gave the students some time to practice rereading. "Now, will you quickly share with a friend nearby? Show the part and talk about what the author did to paint a vivid picture."

Go back to your own reading now, and as you find those really vivid parts, read them again and again to get ready to share in book clubs."

SESSION 7: AUTHORS PAINT PICTURES WITH WORDS

SHARE

Sharing Author's Craft

"READERS, I know you are so excited to share the things you have noticed the author of your series do to paint a picture with words. I bet you've found lots of the same kinds of things we discovered Mary Pope Osborne does in her Magic Tree House book. Thumbs up if that's true!" Many of the kids signaled they agreed. "Let's reread our list to remember those special craft moves authors make to paint with words." I led the class through a choral read of the "How Do Authors Paint Pictures with Words?" chart.

"When you share a part from your book that you could really *see*, be sure to read it out loud to your club so you can all think and talk about what the author did. When you are done talking about one part, a different member can share another part. Go ahead and get started."

I listened in to a club and then voiced over to the class, "Readers, I just heard a club member, over here, who was reading *Arthur's Honey Bear*, notice that when Lillian Hoban said that Arthur decided to sell his old toys in a tag sale, she didn't just say, 'He brought all this stuff out to the curb and set up a tag sale.' No. She instead listed the exact stuff, and the stuff gives readers a feel for Arthur. He brought out his china horse, his yo-yo, his Noah's ark, his Old Maid cards, his rocks, and his marbles. That's why they loved that part, because you could really *see* the whole list of cool things that he brought. Keep going in your clubs."

I then circulated to a few more clubs, coaching in and voicing over little tips such as, "Can you hear your partner? No? Ask her to speak up." Or, "Remember to talk about what the author did to help you paint that picture in your mind."

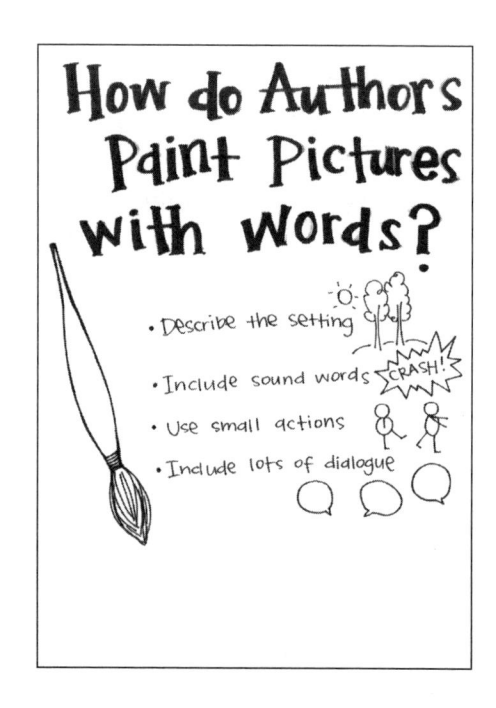

How do Authors Paint Pictures with Words?

- Describe the setting
- Include sound words
- Use small actions
- Include lots of dialogue

Session 8

Authors Use Precise Words

MINILESSON

CONNECTION

Tell children two stories—one with little detail and one with great detail—and ask them to tell you which gives the clearer picture.

"Readers, I'm going to tell you two stories. I want you to tell me which story gives you a clearer picture—story one or story two. Are you ready? Close your eyes and picture this." I watched as the children slowly, with a bit of hesitancy, closed their eyes, and then I began.

"Here is story one. Listen closely, 'You're at the park. It is a nice day. You're playing with your friend. You get hungry. The two of you eat ice cream.' Okay, eyes open! Did you picture it? Did you see it clearly?" Some students nodded, while others gave me a thumbs up. A few students gave me the "somewhat" sign and shook their hands back and forth.

"Okay, now for story two. Listen to see if this story gives a *clearer* picture or a *less* clear picture. Close your eyes, again." I paused and gave students another chance to listen.

"'You're at a WATER PARK. The sun is shining so brightly that you are dripping with sweat. You and your friend are sitting on top of the biggest waterslide in the whole park. All of a sudden, the two of you swoosh down the curvy tunnels until you make an enormous splash into the pool! 'Cowabunga!' you both scream. Then, you hear your stomach grumbling. 'It's time for a snack,' you say as you pull your friend's arm and head to the ice-cream stand. The two of you sit down to share a triple-chocolate ice-cream sundae with whipped cream and a cherry on top. Before you know it, there's chocolate ice cream all over your face! Yum!'" I paused and then told everyone to open their eyes.

"So, which story had a clearer picture—story one or story two?" Fingers shot up toward the ceiling. Students began shouting out, "Two! Two!"

IN THIS SESSION, you'll teach children that readers pay close attention to the words that authors choose to know what is happening in a story.

GETTING READY

- Prepare to tell a story twice, once with few details and once with many (see Connection).
- Display, perhaps on a document camera, pages from the class series book. We use "Alone" from *Days with Frog and Toad* (see Teaching).
- Display pages from the class read-aloud text. We use "The Pudding Like a Night on the Sea" from *The Stories Julian Tells* by Ann Cameron (see Teaching).
- Prepare a copy of the second, more detailed story from Connection to show to the children (see Active Engagement).
- Start a new anchor chart, "Series Readers Become Experts on Author's Craft," and be prepared to add the strategy Post-its, "Notice how the author helps you make vivid pictures in your mind" and "Use the author's precise words to understand the story better" (see Link).

Ask children to turn and talk about why the second story gives a clearer picture. Then share out what they notice, pointing out that they have named the things the class came up with yesterday.

"Why? What gives story two a clearer picture? Turn and talk." As students talked, I listened in to what they were saying. Most of them were recounting the things that we had studied and written down on our one-day chart the day before.

"You are naming some of the same things that we saw yesterday. There's dialogue and small actions and lots of things to get you to see, taste, and hear things in story two! And yes, just like when you write stories, sometimes the clearer picture has more words. Not just *any* words! Words that help you *see* what is happening.

"Authors do the same thing in series. They use *lots* of words to craft and paint the pictures that they want readers to see."

❖ **Name the teaching point.**

"Today I want to teach you that the authors of your series use not just any words, but *precise* words to create really clear pictures in the reader's mind. Readers need to pay close attention to the words that authors choose to know exactly what is happening and how things are happening in their stories."

TEACHING

Read aloud the beginning of a Frog and Toad story and ask children to name any words the author chose to show *how* things are happening. Explain how the words do this.

"Let's look at the words that Arnold Lobel chose to help us think about what is happening in the beginning of the story 'Alone.' I placed the first page under the document camera and said, "Read with me,"

> Toad hurried back to the river. "Frog," he shouted, "it's me. It's your best friend, Toad!"
>
> Frog was too far away to hear. Toad took off his jacket and waved it like a flag. Frog was too far away to see. Toad shouted and waved, but it was no use.

"Do you notice any words that seem to be chosen to show not only what is happening, but how? I do! You see how Arnold Lobel chose the word *shouted*? He didn't just say, *said*. He chose a word that showed *how* Frog speaks. Do you notice any other word choices the author made to show us how something in the story is happening?"

"Waved it like a flag?" a student asked, a little uncertainly.

"You bet. The author wants you to know exactly how Toad was waving his jacket. This shows how frantic Toad is acting. The author chose *waved it like a flag* and the word *shouted* to show that Toad was desperate and wants Frog's attention. He wants Frog to know that he is there and that he doesn't have to be alone, anymore."

The start of the lesson is a mini-inquiry, to introduce students to thinking about precise words. Notice how I use a contrasting example to make obvious how precise words help to make a clearer picture in your mind.

You will see that I first use Alone *by Arnold Lobel, a lower-level text. This way, the text is both easy to read for the students and the craft will "pop out" more. I then move to use Ann Cameron's story "The Pudding Like a Night on the Sea" for two reasons. First, it gives students a second opportunity to notice and think about craft, thus transferring the concept to another text. It also offers an opportunity to work in a text that is harder. This way when students go back to their own texts they have had practice with a variety of complexity levels.*

Display a passage from another read-aloud text and identify some words the author chose to show how things are happening. Explain how.

I replaced this story with a chapter from our read-aloud text, "The Pudding Like a Night on the Sea" and said, "Let's try this again. Remember, here, in "The Pudding Like a Night on the Sea," when the father begins to make the pudding? Let's reread this part together and think about the words this author chose to show us what and how things are happening."

> *Then he took down a knife and sliced five lemons in half. He squeezed the first one. Juice squirted in my eye. "Stand back!" he said and squeezed again. The seeds flew out on the floor.*

"Wow, the words Ann Cameron chose to write here really *show* what is happening." I began to act out each of the words, saying, "Notice that he doesn't cut or chop—he sliced. Can you see him doing that? And the juice didn't just go in Julian's eyes—it squirted. That shows how, exactly, it got in his eyes. And 'The seeds flew.' I can see those seeds flying all over the place!

"Did you see those things as well? Do you see how those precise words help show not just *what* happened but precisely *how*? When you are reading, you should know exactly what is happening—not just generally, but specifically. The words and language that an author chooses will help you."

ACTIVE ENGAGEMENT

Reread the detailed story you shared during the connection and invite children to put up a finger for any precise word they hear that shows how something in the story happens.

I put the text of the detailed story I had read out loud during the connection under the document camera. "Here is story two, which I read to you earlier. Let's reread it and this time, let's be on the alert for precise words. If you see a word that really helps to show more, put one finger up. If you see two words that do that, put two fingers up. And so on. Are you ready? Let's read it together."

> *You're at a WATER PARK. The sun is shining so brightly that you are dripping with sweat. You and your friend are sitting on top of the biggest waterslide in the whole park. All of a sudden, the two of you swoosh down the curvy tunnels until you make an enormous splash into the pool! "Cowabunga!" you both scream. Then, you hear your stomach grumbling. "It's time for a snack." you say as you pull your friend's arm and head to the ice-cream stand. The two of you sit down to share a triple-chocolate ice-cream sundae with whipped cream and a cherry on top. Before you know it, there's chocolate ice cream all over your face! Yum!"*

"Now, turn and talk about what precise words I chose—remember, I'm the author of this story!—to help give you a clear picture and to help you see not just *what* happens, but *how*." I leaned in as children talked and collected several responses. Then I pulled the group back to share out some of their thinking.

SESSION 8: AUTHORS USE PRECISE WORDS

"The Pudding Like a Night on the Sea" is introduced in Session 1 of the Read-Aloud. You'll want to have read this chapter together, laying a foundation of knowledge before you and your students focus on the author's craft. You could, of course, substitute another text your class is familiar with.

While the sessions in this bend ask children to slow down and look carefully at the author's craft, the purpose here is to not just have students notice this craft, but to use it to support their reading. Attending to the precise language an author uses will help readers to envision the text in more detail, strengthening their comprehension.

'So, I heard some of you say that I used the word *dripping* to show that not only are you sweating, you are sweating *a lot*! And others pointed out that the words *swoosh* and *curvy* show *how* you go down the slide. And I heard someone point out the word *scream* shows that you and your friend are both really excited.

"Do you see that *all* authors use really precise words to get readers to see *more*? When you pay close attention to these words, you can see and say exactly what is happening in a story, how characters are feeling and acting, and anything else the author wants you to see."

LINK

Remind children of the strategy they learned today and set them up to read, on the rug, on the lookout for precise words.

"So, readers, as you go off to read your series books, remember, you can study the way your author helps you make a vivid picture in your mind. And you can also pay attention to the author's *precise* words, using them to help you better understand what's going on in your book. This will give you a *lot* to share with your book club." Revealing the new anchor chart for the bend, I added the first two strategies.

"Let's get started, right here and now. Open your book and start reading. When you notice precise words—specially chosen words that help you see how things are happening in your book—pause and think, 'What is the author showing me in this part?' After you have a clear picture in your mind, read on!"

ANCHOR CHART

Series Readers Become
Experts on Author's Craft

- Notice how the author helps you make vivid pictures in your mind.
- Use the author's precise words to understand your story better.

As students started to read in the meeting area, I circulated, listening in. I spent a minute or so with a handful of students. I listened to these kids read and talk about what they were picturing, then I voiced over things that they were finding. 'Hudson just found the word *snapped*. The character didn't just say something, she snapped. She said it quickly and with a little sass. Caroline saw that her author used the word *five* to show not just that there was a snowball fight but precisely *how many* snowballs the character threw."

"Your minds are creating art! Keep picturing your stories and collecting information about your characters, series, *and* authors. The more you know, the more you will be able to talk about with your book club later! Quickly and quietly, return to your seats and keep reading."

CONFERRING AND SMALL-GROUP WORK

Moving Students into Books with Greater Text Complexity

YOU WILL FIND that this unit is a great opportunity to both launch students forward into reading more complex texts as well as support students in how to navigate some of the new complexities they are finding in their books. As your students move up the ladder of text complexity, they will require different kinds of support. Supports that may have been present at easier levels will no longer be as helpful. For example, students will need to depend less on pictures as they move up into chapter books.

Introduce small groups of readers to a new, slightly harder series with a book talk and then provide support as necessary for students to navigate the higher text complexity.

One way to move your second graders up that ladder is to introduce them to a series that is just a notch harder than what they have been reading. The fact that children will be reading within a club of others who are sharing the same books, the same series, will help, and the reader's work with one book in the series will scaffold his or her work with other books in the series. Pulling small groups of students who are reading at similar levels to support their reading in a series will be important to do.

By today, you may therefore want to do some series introductions to help readers with a new series.

Before doing this, look over the series that a group of readers will be moving into and think about the challenges and supports they may encounter in that new series. For example, if you are introducing Horrible Harry books to a group, you may say, "This series is about Harry and many of his friends—Song Lee, Doug, Miss Mackle the teacher, and so on. It is important to know that Doug is the storyteller—that can be a bit confusing sometimes. These kids are in second grade, and you are going to find that Harry is a jokester and there is always some trouble that Harry gets into that his friends help him out of. Let's read the back cover of *this* book and find out about what the trouble will be." You will want to coach into the first few pages. Then you may leave the group to finish the first two chapters.

Afterward, you may return to the same group of readers to have a short book talk about what they learned. Then say, "So you all will go on to finish this book. You probably will finish it in a couple of days and then you can talk about it more. Then we will see what things in *this* Horrible Harry book will be the same in the whole series!"

One thing that will help you in this unit is to read and become familiar with at least one book in every series you have available to your students. Then you will know enough about the series to help children with the supports and challenges.

MID-WORKSHOP TEACHING
Noticing and Tackling New Vocabulary Words

"Readers, as you pay closer attention to the precise words the author of your series chose, some of you are encountering new vocabulary words—words that you have never seen before. Certainly, some of the words that your author chose may be brand-new to you. You know, I bet the author chose those harder words to teach you new vocabulary as you read. Clever!

"Just like you did in nonfiction books, as soon as you notice a new word, you will want to pause and answer the question, 'What does this word mean?' Remember, you can do a few things: You can read on a bit in your story to see if the author gives you more information about the word. You can think about what kind of word it is and what it is similar to. You can also think about what it looks like and give different examples of the word. Doing this will help you become even more of an expert! It will help you understand *all* the words your series author uses."

SESSION 8: AUTHORS USE PRECISE WORDS

You will also want to support students with the various things that may prove to be especially difficult for them in their series. The teaching you are doing in this bend invites kids to engage in a second-grade version of close reading, and that work can be helpful to many of your students. You'll probably find as your second graders move into books that are levels L and M that many of those books will provide less picture support than books at lower levels. Your children are therefore expected, as readers, to visualize in their own minds as they read, which makes the work of studying how the author paints a picture even more important. You'll want to remind them to make mental pictures as they read. Part of this will mean coaching them to really study any pictures that do appear in the text, in addition to making mental pictures from the text, such as where the character is and what the character looks like (what are her facial expressions and body positions?). You may also want to point out to your second graders that they may find that, as they move toward harder and harder books, the pictures will say one thing and the words will say another thing. "Alone" is an example, and you could invite the kids to study it for this reason.

If you decide to do that, you might cover the picture on page 53 and ask students to reread these words: "Toad looked through the windows. He looked in the garden. He did not see Frog."

You could say to the small group of students, "Now, make a picture in your mind: What do you see happening here? Who is in this part? And where? What is he doing?" You might ask members of the small group to talk about that in partnerships.

Readers who know the story will picture Toad standing on the porch of Frog's house, and they'll picture Toad reading a note pinned to Frog's door. Then you could direct readers to the picture and ask what they notice. The picture doesn't show the entire scene, just a snippet of what has already happened. You can point out, "That will happen a lot in your books. If you look to the picture to grasp what is happening in the story, you'll often see only a part of the story." Then, as always, it will be important for the members of the small group to quickly move to trying this in their own books while you coach them.

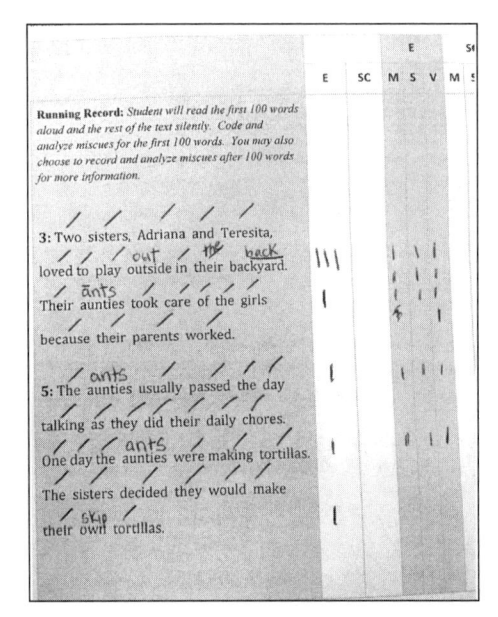

FIG. 8–1 Miscue Analysis of a J Running Record. It is still important to study how students are developing word-solving skills. This running record shows how the reader doesn't attend to the endings of words or self-correct—an important goal to help readers reinforce and solidify before moving into more complex texts.

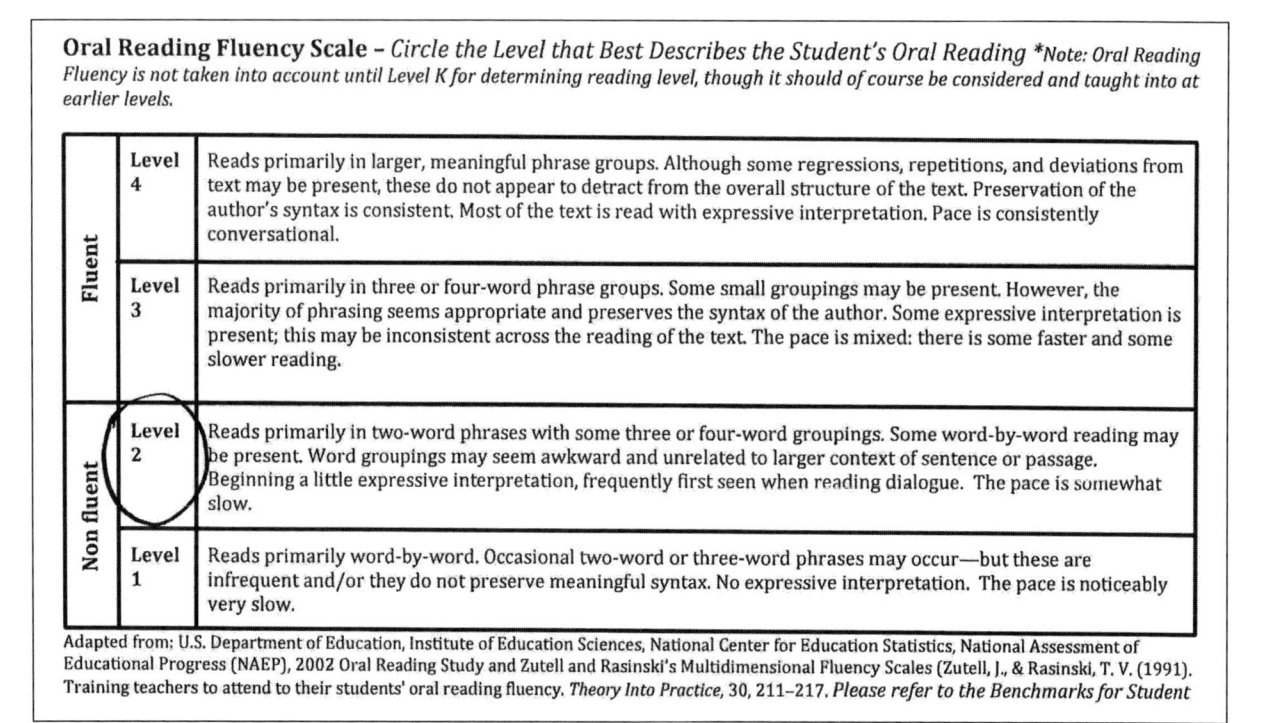

Oral Reading Fluency Scale – *Circle the Level that Best Describes the Student's Oral Reading* *Note: Oral Reading Fluency is not taken into account until Level K for determining reading level, though it should of course be considered and taught into at earlier levels.*

	Level	
Fluent	Level 4	Reads primarily in larger, meaningful phrase groups. Although some regressions, repetitions, and deviations from text may be present, these do not appear to detract from the overall structure of the text. Preservation of the author's syntax is consistent. Most of the text is read with expressive interpretation. Pace is consistently conversational.
Fluent	Level 3	Reads primarily in three or four-word phrase groups. Some small groupings may be present. However, the majority of phrasing seems appropriate and preserves the syntax of the author. Some expressive interpretation is present; this may be inconsistent across the reading of the text. The pace is mixed: there is some faster and some slower reading.
Non fluent	Level 2	Reads primarily in two-word phrases with some three or four-word groupings. Some word-by-word reading may be present. Word groupings may seem awkward and unrelated to larger context of sentence or passage. Beginning a little expressive interpretation, frequently first seen when reading dialogue. The pace is somewhat slow.
Non fluent	Level 1	Reads primarily word-by-word. Occasional two-word or three-word phrases may occur—but these are infrequent and/or they do not preserve meaningful syntax. No expressive interpretation. The pace is noticeably very slow.

Adapted from: U.S. Department of Education, Institute of Education Sciences, National Center for Education Statistics, National Assessment of Educational Progress (NAEP), 2002 Oral Reading Study and Zutell and Rasinski's Multidimensional Fluency Scales (Zutell, J., & Rasinski, T. V. (1991). Training teachers to attend to their students' oral reading fluency. *Theory Into Practice*, 30, 211–217. *Please refer to the Benchmarks for Student*

FIG. 8–2 Fluency Scale from a J Running Record. At level J and above, the running record asks teachers to also note the specifics about the reader's level of fluency. This is another place to establish specific goals for readers.

SHARE

Analyzing Important Parts of a Story

Set children up to talk, first with a partner and then with their club, about important parts of their books and how the author uses precise words to help readers learn something from those parts.

"Readers, before you get together with your club, look over what you just read and share it with your partners first. Think about your story and a part that is really important. This might be a part where the character has a strong feeling—maybe she is encountering a problem or there is a big change happening. When you have the part in mind, Partner 1, you share first. Both of you, Partners A and B, listen and think about the precise words that help you see more and know more about that section. Think about what is important that you are learning about this story."

As I circulated, I noticed what parts students were sharing, listened to the ideas and words that they shared, and heard them read selected parts out loud. Each time I listened to a partnership and gave them a quick tip, I voiced over that tip to the whole class. I said, "Don't just choose *any* word. Choose a word that shows not just what is happening but *how*," and "Partners, make sure you agree with what your partner is saying. Ask them, 'Would you read me that part again?' or 'Why do you think that is important to this part?' Remember, the two of you are helping one another get ready to share in your book club!"

After both partners have had a chance to talk about the important parts of their books and what the language in it showed, I said, "Now, partners, join up with the rest of your club to share those same parts and any new ideas you have. Listen to the language in one another's parts to see if you can say more about that part. *Then*—and here is the big thing to think about—look into your own book to see if you *too* have a similar part or idea.

"Make sure everyone gets a chance to share their ideas. Go ahead!"

FIG. 8–3 A book club shares craft moves they noticed the author make in their series books.

Session 9

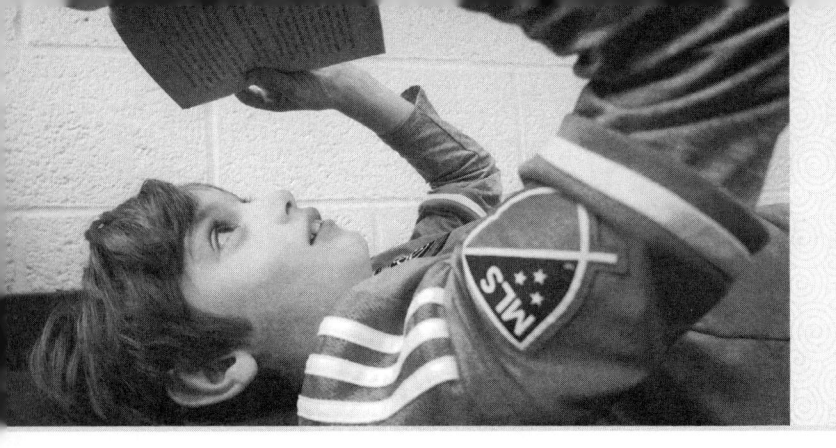

Authors Use Literary Language to Make the Ordinary Extraordinary

IN THIS SESSION, you'll teach children that another craft move that readers notice is the author's use of literary language. Readers notice the words authors choose to make simple things *extraordinary*, and they figure out what the author really means.

GETTING READY

- Display the anchor chart from the previous unit of study, "Understanding Literary Language," so that it is ready to refer to (see Connection and Active Engagement).
- Reread a couple pages of a familiar read-aloud that include literary language. We suggest using the first two pages of "The Pudding Like a Night on the Sea" from *The Stories Julian Tells* by Ann Cameron (see Teaching and Active Engagement and Conferring and Small-Group Work).
- Display the anchor chart "Series Readers Become Experts on Author's Craft" and be prepared to add the strategy—"Think about extraordinary language (Ask, 'What does it really mean?')" (see Link).
- Ask students to bring their book to meeting area with artful craft marked (see Share).

MINILESSON

CONNECTION

Remind children of their literary language study from earlier in the year, and bring out the chart you made to understand literary language.

"Readers, earlier this year, you studied the literary language that authors use." I pulled out a familiar chart to remind students of the strategies they had learned. "Will you quickly turn to your partner and remind each other of what readers can do to study special language in books. You can use the chart to help you remember all that you've learned." I leaned in to listen as partners shared.

ANCHOR CHART

Understanding Literary Language

- Pay attention to special language.
  1. Notice when words are used in special ways.
  2. Reread that part.
  3. Remember what's going on in the story.
  4. Think, 'What special meaning does the author want me to get?'
- When two things are compared, think about how they're alike.
- Figure out what playful language REALLY means.

I listened as children reviewed and talked about the chart. Then I said, "Wowie! You all are total experts on literary language! So here is my question—have you been noticing literary language in your series?"

When one child said no, I fell backward in shock. "Bradley—you have got to be kidding," I said, floored that he could possibly say he hadn't been continuing to draw on all the class had learned earlier. "You know *so much*, and you definitely want to remember to use all you know."

❖ **Name the teaching point.**

"Today I want to teach you that when readers study an author's craft, they pay attention to the words that an author has used. Readers notice ways in which authors use words to make even a simple, ordinary thing be *extraordinary*, and they wonder, 'What does the author really mean?'"

What is true about this one student is most likely true about many of the students in your class. As you teach each day, you will want to be sure that students are carrying the teaching and learning that they did in previous units as well as earlier in this unit. Their stories may be more complex, and it may be difficult to orchestrate previously-taught skills. This is a good reason to revisit these skills and reinforce these strategies across the year.

TEACHING

Reread part of the read-aloud text, this time showing children the ways the author uses language to compare things and to make things sound extraordinary.

"Readers, the really important thing for you to notice is that an author can take some plain ol' regular thing and choose just the right words to make it sound extraordinary. Like, Ann Cameron, the author of *The Stories Julian Tells*, could have written, 'He laughed,' but instead she wrote this":

When he laughs, the sun laughs in the windowpanes.

"Tell me something. Did the sun *really* laugh? No, of course not! But the author, she wanted us to know what it felt like when the father laughed, and so she compared his laughter to the bright sun. Here's another comparison she made. Listen":

We felt like two leaves in a storm.

"Hmm, I wonder what she is trying to say when she says the kids felt like two leaves in a storm. Right now, picture a bunch of leaves in a storm—what happens to them? What's life like for a leaf in a storm? Right now, sitting where you are, will you pretend to be a leaf, and pretend great hurricane winds are blowing around you?" The children shivered and shook, and I generated words, such as *shake* and *tremble*, to capture what I saw.

"Do you see how noticing the literary language the author uses makes us picture even more? We can't walk away from this story just picturing leaves shaking in a rainstorm. No, no, no! We have to imagine what the author wants us to see. Here, she wants us to see, the children shaking and trembling because their dad is angry. Their dad, the storm!"

Here I make sure that I show students several examples. This is important because I am not trying to teach one particular saying or metaphor or idiom. I am trying to show students how to notice this language in their own books and to monitor their understanding.

For many students this will be hard work. Some readers zip through their texts, while other students read more literally. This work calls for readers to read thoughtfully and draw inferences. Others may have difficulty because of a language barrier. Idioms and metaphors and other types of literary language usually are mostly acquired by English language learners in the last stages of language acquisition. This lesson will begin to provide the scaffolding you'll need to offer students in the earlier stages of language acquisition who are reading books with a lot of literary language.

ACTIVE ENGAGEMENT

Set children up to continue to marvel at the literary language in the text, thinking about what the words show the reader. Ask them to find exact lines and say what they think the author really means.

"Listen to this part of Ann Cameron's story to see if you can notice the literary language. Think to yourself, 'What is the author trying to show?'" I said and read:

When he thinks, you can almost see his thoughts sitting on all the tables and chairs.

"What is she trying to show? What does this *really* mean?" I gestured toward the "Understanding Literary Language" chart. "Who has some ideas? Turn and tell your partner."

I coached in to help students think about what this might mean. "This partnership, over here, they think that the author is trying to show that Julian and Huey's father is *really* thoughtful. He not only laughs hard but he also thinks hard, too. Do you agree? Ann didn't use just ordinary words like, 'Dad thought about really important things for a long time.' Nope! She wrote, 'When he thinks, you can almost see his thoughts sitting on all the tables and chairs.' How extraordinary!" The students and I located another passage, this time talking about Ann Cameron's description of the father's eyes, "his eyes like black lightning," to give students another opportunity to practice and think about the literary language in the text.

LINK

Send children off to read, reminding them to pay close attention to and mark literary language to study and talk about in their book clubs.

"So, readers, as you go off to read, you will want to study the language the author uses. Pay special attention to the words the author chose, especially when the author compares two things." I added a new strategy to the anchor chart.

"When you see extraordinary language in your books, use a Post-it to mark the amazing, extraordinary parts! And remember to think, 'What does this *really* mean? What does the author want to show?' Then jot that down. Those things, too, can be a great source of conversation in your book clubs.

"My guess is that as you read not just one book in your series, but *all* the books in your series, you are going to see these things in *many* of those books. Okay, readers, off you go!"

Think about the extraordinary language
"We felt like two leaves in a storm."

Ask, "What does it really mean?"
The boys feel scared

CONFERRING AND SMALL-GROUP WORK

Conducting Coaching Conferences around Literary Language

TODAY YOU MAY DECIDE to check in on readers to make certain that they are drawing on all they know to try to figure out the meaning of literary language. You may want to check your running records to see if you have readers hovering (or perhaps, lingering) around levels J and K. You may want to conduct coaching conferences with these readers. Sitting close, listen to the reader and coach in as needed, offering lean prompts and reactions to their reading. You may hear yourself saying things like "Whoa! His *eyes were peeled*? He is really paying close attention. He must be feeling excited" when the reader gets to a bit of figurative phrasing. Coaching in as students read helps them to monitor and read on the lookout for similar phrases they may be reading right by without much thought.

Before students begin to understand literary language, they need to monitor for sense enough to realize that the phrase is confusing. You'll want your readers to get in the habit of pausing every so often to ask themselves if they really understand what the author is saying. Celebrate the approximations students make. You'll want your readers to notice extraordinary phrases and come up with several tentative theories as to what they could mean. This helps to foster a sense of curiosity about language and a willingness to do the deep thinking these passages require.

Check in with ongoing small groups.

If you supported a small group of students yesterday, you may want to work with that group again. Remember that you'll want to lighten your scaffolds. If you introduced a new series to children reading at lower levels, you might want to pull this group together again to introduce a second book. Your book introduction will likely be shorter than yesterday. You may ask students to give each other a quick preview of the book, and then help them look through the text to discuss words and phrases that might be tricky.

Alternatively you might reconvene a strategy group, reminding them of what you worked on yesterday and asking them to take out their books and get started in doing that work right away. For example, if you choose to meet with a group working on visualizing, you'll want to observe these readers as they try out this work with greater independence. Move from reader to reader, asking students to pause and describe what they are picturing in their minds. You may want to prompt for more information asking "Why?" or "How do you know?" to better understand the way the reader is noticing the language of the text.

MID-WORKSHOP TEACHING
Working through Possible Meanings of Literary Language

"Readers, eyes on me. Some of you are studying the extraordinary language in your series books and having a hard time thinking about what it at it might mean. Sometimes, I might try to think about a *few* things it *could* mean and then decide which matches best with what is happening.

"So, in this part, where Julian's father finds them under the bed and the author wrote, 'his eyes like black lightning,' maybe the author wants me to know that his eyes were really shining and bright and beautiful. *Or* she wants me to know that they are scary and frightening, like how lightning is sometimes. *Or* she wants me to know that his eyes are really hot like the room is hot. Wait, no, that doesn't make any sense. The one that fits best is that she is trying to show how mad Julian's father is and how scared the kids are.

"Right now, look back at some literary language that you found. Consider a *couple* possibilities to either confirm your initial thought or to help you clarify what it might mean. During your book club time, check to see if the other members of your club agree with your ideas.

SESSION 9: AUTHORS USE LITERARY LANGUAGE TO MAKE THE ORDINARY EXTRAORDINARY

SHARE

Listening to Literary Language

Gather students in a circle so that they can see and hear each other while they share examples of literary language.

"Readers, look over the artful craft that you marked in your books. Find the best, most beautiful, most extraordinary language that your author used. And then come to the meeting area and make a large circle." I gave the class a minute to settle on the rug.

"We are going to share and listen to all the marvelous ways our authors are using language in extraordinary, beautiful ways. You will each take a turn reading aloud a line you found in your book. We won't clap; we will just listen to the language. After one person shares, anyone can go next. If you don't hear someone speaking, it could mean that it's your turn. I will let you decide. Just be respectful and don't talk 'on top' of someone else. Let's be really good listeners."

Send students off to meet with their clubs to discuss literary language from their series books.

After everyone had shared, I said to the students, "Those lines were so beautiful. Such extraordinary language! But, to really become an expert and understand what all of these lines mean, it helps to know the story better. Right now, you'll spend some time with your club members, discussing the craft you noticed and thought about. Remember, if you have found some extraordinary language, ask one another, 'What does this *really* mean? What do you think that the author is trying to show?' If your friend has a hard time answering, what should you do?"

"Help them!" the class shouted in unison.

"Yes, work together. You can reread together to think about what the author is trying to show. If the author is comparing two things, you might ask, 'How are these two things alike?' Then, you can work together to understand why the author chose to use *those* words. Go ahead expert series readers! Off you go into your clubs!"

Session 10

Authors Think about How Whole Stories—and Series—Will Go

MINILESSON

In your connection, you might begin by describing a typical school day, inviting children to help you fill in the details. Leaving spaces for children to fill in, say, "Whenever you come to school in the morning, you know that the first thing you'll do is . . . And once everything is away, we gather on the rug for . . . And later in the day, you go to lunch and then comes . . ." Then, connect the way kids can anticipate how the school day will go to the way readers anticipate how a story will go. You might go on to say, "You see there's a way that our school day tends to go." I gestured toward the daily agenda on the wall. "It's a lot like your series books. Once you have read the first book, you will start to know how the other books in the series will tend to go."

Name the teaching point. Say, "Today I want to teach you that when readers study an author's craft, they don't just notice the way the author uses words and language. They also notice the way the *whole* story tends to go. And once readers get to know a series particularly well, they can start a new book in the series and think, 'Oh yeah, I know how this book is going to go because I know how the series goes!'"

During the teaching, you will want to revisit a couple of stories that students know well. Using *Days with Frog and Toad* may be best, because the stories are short and highly repetitive. You might say, "We are going to see if Arnold Lobel wrote the Frog and Toad stories so that they tend to go the same way." You might say, "If I was to describe how these stories tend to go—how they often start off, what usually happens in the middle, and how they usually end, I might say, 'The stories usually start off with Toad causing some sort of problem or having a hard time. Things usually get worse before they get better, and in the end Frog often helps him out.' Do you agree with me?" Then I might open the book to a few stories, like "The Kite" and "Alone" to just confirm that this *is* how many of these stories go.

Then I would say to readers, "If I was to read a *new* story, like, 'Down the Hill,' which is about Frog and Toad going sledding, I can guess how the whole story might go. Toad will not want to go sledding because he will be too scared. Frog will get him to go, maybe even trick him. Toad will go sledding and will be really scared, maybe even crash the sled. Frog will find him in the end and make him laugh somehow."

Be sure to debrief what you did in front of the students. You might say, "Did you see how I can think about how the author writes a *whole* story? I can use that to help me think about how to get ready for the next story. When I read a new story in the series, I can really make good predictions about what will happen and how the story will go." You might even read the beginning of the story, to see if any of your predictions are true.

During the active engagement, you'll want to coach children to practice noticing what the author does to make the stories in a series go the same way. You may decide to turn to another familiar series. For instance, you may reread the opening pages of a couple of Magic Tree House books, Cam Jansen books, or Junie B. Jones books, asking students to turn and talk about the way these stories tend to go. By reading aloud a few beginnings, students can see how these stories are similarly structured and that books in a series are very predictable in how they "tend to go." In fact, that's what links the books together as a series.

In your link, you might say "Readers, you're becoming strong at finding *lots* of things that your authors do to make their series so much fun to read. Impressive! Not only can you think about craft moves your authors use across the series, you can also use what you know about how your author writes one story in a series to help you predict how new stories in that series will go! Finding the things that are the same across your books helps you pay closer attention to what is happening in your stories."

Remind your readers of what they can do as they read on in their series or as they start new ones. Take out the anchor chart and add the next bullet. Remind your readers that they will be meeting in clubs at the share session, so they should be on the lookout for things to share.

ANCHOR CHART

Series Readers Become
Experts on Author's Craft

- Notice how the author helps you make vivid pictures in your mind.
- Use the author's precise words to understand the story better.
- Think about the extraordinary language (Ask, "What does it really mean?").
- **Predict how your story will go, using what you know about the other stories in the series.**

Predict how the story will go, using what you know about the other stories in the series

CONFERRING AND SMALL-GROUP WORK

As you confer and pull small groups, you will want to assess and think about supporting students with specific skills to help them read and understand their stories better. While your students work with great enthusiasm on the brand-new work of studying series, you, of course, will keep in mind that actually, their work is not brand-new at all. This unit provides them with yet one more continued opportunity to develop all their skills as readers. And it will be important for your teaching to be informed mostly by your ongoing attention to your students' progress along skill trajectories that you've been supporting for the entire year.

Today, then, you may decide to deliberately work with kids in skill-based groups that cut across their series groups. That is, you no doubt have a number of kids who have been working on reading with increasing fluency, on becoming more resourceful word solvers, or on being able to retell a story, using story elements to help them. Today might be a good day to gather some of those students and to remind them that they need to continue doing that work even as they read series. You could return to the skill-based groups that you instituted toward the end of your previous unit, reminding students to continue the work they were doing within those groups.

Mid-Workshop Teaching

During the mid-workshop teaching, nudge kids to think about the work have they done, so far, in their new book. You might say, "How many of you are finding that the way you thought the story was *going* to go is actually going that way so far? How many of you are finding that what you thought would happen *isn't* happening? Sometimes we will be right, and other times we need to revise, or change, our thinking."

SHARE

For today's share, you might suggest that clubs share the things that they noticed about how their books tend to go and talk about whether this holds true for all the books in a series. You might say, "Share how you think the stories in your series tend to go and try to say how you know. Each of your club mates will then think, 'Do I agree?'"

You may let your clubs get started with that and share the ideas that they come up with. Then you may pause the groups and voice over to everyone, "After you share how your series tends to go and everyone mostly agrees, then one of you can share what you think is going to happen next, specifically in your book. Club mates, your job is to listen and think about if you agree or not. Does that make sense? If it doesn't, help your club mate come up with a *better* prediction." Encourage your students to get started. You may decide to voice over a few examples of how clubs are working together to clarify one another's ideas as well as give suggestions of how to make those ideas even stronger.

Session 11

Authors Have Ways to Bring Stories to Life

IN THIS SESSION, you'll teach children that readers listen for author's craft in the words the author uses and look for it in how the author places the words on the page so that they know how to read like storytellers.

GETTING READY

- Select a section from a familiar text that has clear print cues, such as punctuation and special print, to display using a document camera or other device. We suggest using the unit's read-aloud, "The Pudding Like a Night on the Sea" from *The Stories Julian Tells* by Ann Cameron. Create a copy of this portion of the text without any punctuation or line breaks (see Teaching and Active Engagement).
- Display the anchor chart, "Series Readers Become Experts on Author's Craft," and be prepared to add the new strategy Post-it, "Use the punctuation and special print to bring your story to life" (see Teaching and Active Engagement and Link).
- Display the "How Authors Bring a Story to Life" chart (see Link).
- Display a section of text in which punctuation or other print cues help the reader know how to read like a storyteller. We suggest a paragraph in the first story of *The Stories Julian Tells* (see Mid-Workshop Teaching).
- Ask students to bring their books to share with their book clubs (see Share).

MINILESSON

CONNECTION

Tell a story to show children that readers can hear the author's craft in a story by the way it is read aloud or told.

"My grandfather was a great storyteller. He would sit in a big chair and all of the grandchildren would gather around him and he'd tell us story after story. And we'd sit and listen for hours. In a way, he was just like the authors of your series books, except he didn't write his stories down on paper; he wrote them with his voice.

"You see, his stories were amazing and beautiful to listen to because of the way he *told* them. His voice would go UP and down, get LOUD and soft, *speed up* and s-l-o-w down. He used his voice to make his stories come to life, to make them sound the way the authors want them to sound. Authors have ways to help every reader bring stories to life, just the way a storyteller would."

❖ **Name the teaching point.**

"Today I want to teach you that authors craft not just what the words they use, but also the way those words are placed on the page. Authors include signals in the print—like bold or italic font or large type or even teeny tiny things like commas and periods—to tell the reader how they want a story to sound."

TEACHING AND ACTIVE ENGAGEMENT

Read a passage two different ways to demonstrate the how punctuation and special print make the meaning of the text clearer.

"Readers, let's try to read, with our best fluent voices, this part of the story from *The Stories Julian Tells*, without any signals. Let's see if we can do it." Placing the copy of the text on the document camera, I invited the students to read along with me.

> *Where is the pudding my mother said where are you boys my father said his voice went through every crack and corner of the house we felt like two leaves in a storm where are you I said my father's voice was booming Huey whispered to me I'm scared Huey he called Julian*

Pretty soon, we were all laughing. "It's hard right? I mean, who is saying, 'I'm scared'? And is it 'I'm scared Huey.' or is it 'I'm scared. Huey, he called.' It's hard to know, without punctuation. Let's reread it, now, with the punctuation and the special print, to see how it signals us to read differently and how it helps create a clearer picture for us."

Guide children to notice ways that an author tells the reader how a story should sound.

I placed the same portion of text under the document camera and said, "Look for punctuation or bold words or all caps or italics." Then I asked the children to read it to themselves by speaking into their conch shell and to make sure they noticed and followed the signals the author left for them. Throughout the meeting area, children began reading this excerpt quietly to themselves.

> "Where is the pudding?" my mother said.
>
> "WHERE ARE YOU BOYS?" my father said. His voice went through every crack and corner of the house.
>
> We felt like two leaves in a storm.
>
> "WHERE ARE YOU? I SAID!" My father's voice was booming.
>
> Huey whispered to me, "I'm scared."
>
> We heard my father walking slowly through the rooms.
>
> "Huey!" he called. "Julian!"

I allowed enough time for readers to at least notice the text clues, such as capital letters and exclamation points, and begin to figure out their meaning.

"We have to read it differently, don't we? The signals here, the words in capital letters and the punctuation, all tell us that we have to read these parts with more feeling and emphasis. Turn and talk to your partner about how we should read these parts." As children talked to their partners, I listened in, and after a moment I said, "Let me name out a few things that I heard you say. If you saw the same thing, just put your thumb up on your knee. The author, Ann Cameron,

---

Paying attention to punctuation will help your students work on their phrasing as they try to read their books more fluently. You will find that late in second grade, the books that your students are reading have longer and more complex sentences. They will also have more dialogue to negotiate. All in all, you want your students to continue to think about how the story sounds in their mind as they read it. This lesson gives your students this type of practice.

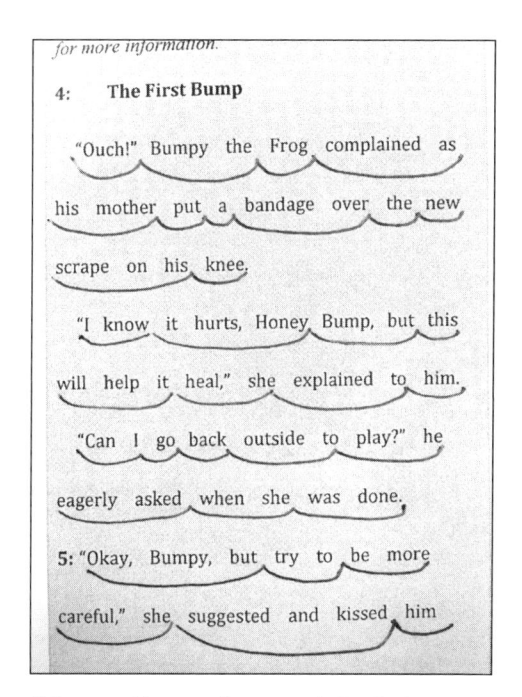

FIG. 11–1 Use running records to study students' fluency. This student reads in one- or two-word phrases (with occasional three-word phrases) and doesn't consistently attend to punctuation. In many cases, syntax is lost, which can affect a student's comprehension of a text.

doesn't use italics to emphasize words she wants you to read with extra strength, but she does use all caps. See here and here?" I pointed those parts out in the text "Why did she do this?"

Several children chimed in, "She wanted to show that the dad was mad." "She shows how the dad is feeling!" "To show us that the dad has a really loud voice!"

"I agree!" other kids said and put their thumbs on their knees.

"I do, too. The author wants us to know that the dad feels angry and is shouting. She even tells us that 'His voice went through every crack and corner.' In other words, the father's voice was *so loud* that it filled the whole house! Wow, that's a *really* loud voice! And, how do we know that the father's voice was angry and not just loud?"

"Because he told the boys not to eat the pudding, and they did!" several students volunteered.

"Right, so we can use what we know about the story to read the signals from the author." I pointed to the punctuation marks and the words in all caps. Then I pointed to the word *whispered*.

"The partnership over here noticed that Ann didn't write, 'said Huey.' Instead, she used the word *whispered*. *Whispered* and *called* both give clues about how to read that dialogue. Last, a bunch of you saw that she uses exclamation points to indicate yelling and saying things with power.

"Now let's remember what we know about the story and try to follow the author's signals one more time to read in a way that brings the story to life and helps us understand the characters."

> *"Where is the pudding?" my mother said.*
>
> *"WHERE ARE YOU BOYS?" my father said. His voice went through every crack and corner of the house.*
>
> *We felt like two leaves in a storm.*
>
> *"WHERE ARE YOU? I SAID!" My father's voice was booming.*
>
> *Huey whispered to me, "I'm scared."*
>
> *"Huey!" he called. "Julian!"*

I added a new point to our anchor chart.

> **ANCHOR CHART**
>
> **Series Readers Become Experts on Author's Craft**
>
> - Notice how the author helps you make vivid pictures in your mind
> - Use the author's precise words to understand the story better
> - Think about the extraordinary language (Ask, "What does it really mean?")
> - Predict how your story will go, using what you know about the other stories in the series
> - **Use the author's punctuation and special print to bring your story to life**

LINK

Guide children to notice ways that an author brings a story to life and list them on a chart for them to use as a reference.

"As you read your series books today, you will look for ways that the author tells you how to bring the story to life. Before you go off to read, let's make a list of some of the signals we have already noticed authors using." Guided by the children's responses, I made a quick list that included exclamation points and question marks, words in all capital letters, and bold print. "When you see an exclamation point, how do you know whether a character is angry or excited? Quickly tell your partner!" After just a few seconds, I called for everyone's attention and confirmed that they knew to also think about what's happening in the story to make the characters sound right.

"What are examples of words that tell you how a character is speaking?" I added words like *whispered*, *laughed*, and *yelled* to the list.

"Use your Post-its to mark places in your book where the author does a good job of telling you how to make the story sound. You will want to make sure you have a few examples of these things marked and ready to share with your clubs during our share session at the end of workshop."

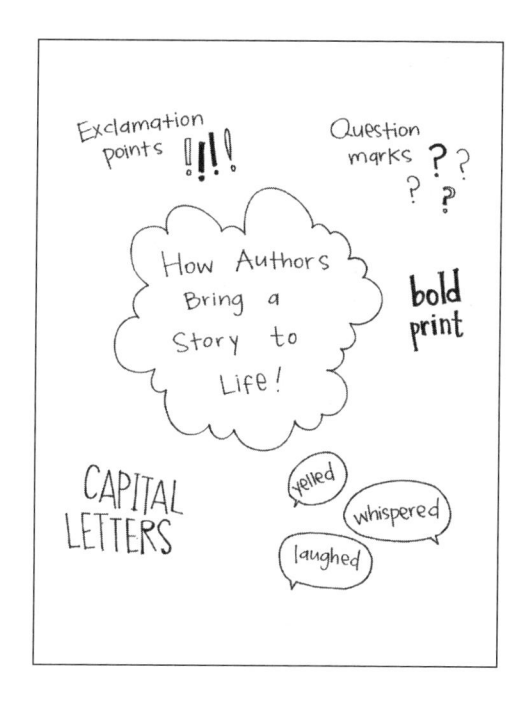

SESSION 11: AUTHORS HAVE WAYS TO BRING STORIES TO LIFE

CONFERRING AND SMALL-GROUP WORK

Supporting Students in the Work They Need to Progress

Continue to support students in noticing author's craft so that they can read analytically.

As you think about your conferring and small-group work for today, you'll probably want to divide your time between supporting individual readers on the work they need to do to progress and the specific work of this unit.

This unit will give your readers a chance to reread books as writers, noticing the craft moves that authors have made. That sort of analytic reading, realizing that authors make decisions on purpose, is a good thing to teach kids from an early age. If your youngsters participate in a writing workshop, they'll be especially able to notice the craft moves that authors have made, and they'll want to emulate those moves in their own writing as well. You'll find that children have very few problems noticing bold font and unusual punctuation but far more problems noticing the patterns that undergird whole books.

Coach below-level readers to problem solve words while they read.

You'll definitely want to devote part of the reading workshop to leading guided reading sessions for your readers who are reading below grade level. This is important because these readers are most likely still learning to orchestrate their word-solving skills in flexible and efficient ways and need to be coached to apply those skills in increasingly complex texts. For example, if you have readers who are reading level G books independently, you'll want to make sure they are working, with support, in level H books across a series of sessions. These readers need multiple opportunities for active word-solving and fluency practice across multiple texts. Choose two or three short level H texts and decide the order in which readers will read these texts. Then plan book introductions that provide less support over time, moving readers closer to independence in the level.

Each ten-minute guided reading session will begin with a short book introduction. In this introduction, you will want to set the readers up to do some problem-solving work.

That means giving them a brief preview of the book by showing the cover and possibly one or two pages of the text, explaining that knowing a little bit about the book will help them rely on meaning as a source of information as they problem solve unfamiliar words. In the text, there may be one or two tricky parts connected to language structure or words that you will want to highlight ahead of time.

Make sure to leave some of these tricky parts for readers to work through as they read. For example, in an introduction to a level H book, *Pepper's Adventure*, you might say, "Readers I brought a book for you to read today called *Pepper's Adventure*. It is about

> **MID-WORKSHOP TEACHING**
> **Paying Attention to Punctuation**
>
> "Many of you are noticing that the authors of your books use all sorts of unusual punctuation. Charlie noticed dashes in his book. He said they helped him to read the sentences better, scooping up the words. Let's look at page 6 from the first story of *The Stories Julian Tells*." I placed the text under the document camera.
>
> > *"Perfect!" he said. "Now I'm going to take a nap. If something important happens, bother me. If nothing important happens, don't bother me. And—the pudding is for your mother. Leave the pudding alone!"*
>
> "Do you see how the author uses the commas to show us how to scoop up those words and read them together? And the dash shows us how to pause, to separate the words on either side of it. When you are reading, don't skip the commas and dashes—or *any* punctuation. Think about why the author included that punctuation, and follow the author's guidance."

Sarah and her two pet mice, Pepper and Salt." You could turn to the first couple pages to show the characters. "One day Nicky, Sarah's neighbor, came over to play. That's when the problem happened with one of the mice." Then turn back to the cover and remind the readers of the title and ask them to predict what the problem will be. They could give you a thumbs up when they have that prediction. You might say, "Okay readers, hold that idea in your mind as you keep track of what happens." Then you might point out a tricky word at the beginning of the story. "Readers, on this page we see that Sarah's mice have a ladder in their cage. Can you locate the word *ladder*?" The readers should point to the word. "What are the two syllables in *ladder*?" The children should say the two syllables as you use your fingers to show each syllable, making sure to point out that *lad* is the first syllable and has a short *a* sound. "There will be other words in this book where you will have to make sure you read each syllable carefully."

You probably won't bring readers to the other words, such as *garden* and *hiding*, which you know could be tricky; rather, you would leave those opportunities for students to do that work in the context of reading.

After the introduction, readers should read independently while you prompt them to use strategies to problem solve words and monitor their reading. In the final minute or two, you'll want to have a short comprehension conversation and provide a teaching point based on your observations and coaching during the session. Children will keep this book in their book baggies so they can reread it with increasing accuracy, fluency, and comprehension. Based on your observations during this guided reading session, you will want to think about how much support readers need in the next book introduction and shorten it accordingly.

SHARE

Performing Parts Like Storytellers

"READERS, it's time to meet in your clubs! Meet in your special club areas. Get together and reread a part or a page aloud so your clubmates can *listen* to the beautiful craft that you found. Then choose a part for your club to perform for another club. You and your club mates can take on different roles to show how that part should sound.

I then circulated among the clubs, listening in to how they read their books. I made sure that clubs quickly decided on the part that they were going to perform. Then I made sure that students not only selected characters to "read" and perform, but that someone represented the narrator's voice as well.

"After you practice reading the part a few times, making it sound better and better, talk about the punctuation and the special print you noticed that helped you read it in a special way. Be an expert! Don't just name *what* the writer did, try to say *why* the author did that. What was the author trying to show?

I then helped students talk about *how* they decided to read parts. I coached in, to get readers to be more critical and thoughtful about their reading. I raised questions such as "Are there other ways to read that part?" and "Why did you read it that way?" and "What did you all think about how that sounded?" I tried to coach the students to ask each other these same questions and consider multiple possibilities. This coaching will help to get more participation, critical thinking, and reading happening in the clubs.

"In a few minutes, I'm going to send your club to perform for another club, so get working—fast!" When the clubs seemed ready to perform their parts, I held up two books, one from each of two different series. "Eyes on me! Will these two clubs please get together right over here!" I repeated the move to pair up the remaining clubs. "Clubs, decide who will read first. Then, bring those stories to life!"

FIG. 11–2 Two readers prepare to perform a part of their book for their club and then for another club.

Session 12

Authors Plan Their Story Endings

MINILESSON

In your connection, you might begin this lesson by retelling a favorite fairy tale that your class knows well, perhaps "The Three Little Pigs" or "Little Red Riding Hood." Whichever story you choose, you will want to dramatize and overemphasize the importance that the ending has to a story. Perhaps your retelling will sound something like this: "We all know the story of Little Red Riding Hood, don't we? Listen to me retell this favorite story of ours. If you *love* the retell I give, give me two thumbs up. If you think I could do a better job, put your thumb on your knee. Here I go. Little Red Riding Hood went to visit her grandmother and even though her mother told her to go straight there, she stopped in the meadow to pick flowers and talked to the big, bad wolf! And then she got to her grandmother's house . . . blah, blah, the end."

Undoubtedly you will see many thumbs on knees, but keep the drama going. Look bewildered and even ask the class, "Why? What could be better?" You should hear a chorus of voices, shouting "You forgot the ending!" Then you will want to say to your students that endings matter—they matter to the stories we read and to the ones we write. You will want to convey to them that endings are not just added to finish a story, but to teach the reader.

Name the teaching point by saying, "Today I want to teach you that readers think carefully at the end of a book, just as they do at the start. Readers think, 'Why did the author choose to end the story this way? Is there an important lesson for me to learn?'"

SESSION 12: AUTHORS PLAN THEIR STORY ENDINGS

71

ANCHOR CHART

Series Readers Become Experts on Author's Craft

- Notice how the author helps you make vivid pictures in your mind.
- Use the author's precise words to understand the story better.
- Think about the extraordinary language (Ask, "What does it really mean?").
- Predict how your story will go, using what you know about the other stories in the series.
- Use the author's punctuation and special print to bring your story to life.
- **Ask, "Why did the author end the book this way? What lesson am I supposed to learn?"**

   During the teaching, show students a selection of endings to stories that you all have read together. You may show them the ending to Frog and Toad's "Alone" or Julian's "The Pudding Like a Night on the Sea" or the first story in the Poppleton series. Whichever story you start with, you will want to show students how to notice the decision the author made to end the story and think out loud as to a possible lesson everyone could learn. Perhaps you will reread one of the stories in *Days with Frog and Toad* such as: "Alone," placing it under the document camera. You may say, "Remember this story and how Toad finally found Frog in the end? It ends with Frog explaining that he just wanted to be alone, but now that Toad was there he was happy to be with him too—even if that meant eating wet sandwiches. That is how the author, Arnold Lobel, ended the story. *But*, now I have to think, why? What lesson does he want us to learn—possibly?" Some of your students may raise their hands. This shows that they are thinking alongside of you. Because you did ask this question out loud, you will want to make sure that you answer the question. You might say, "Listen to see if I had the same thought as you. Maybe the author wrote the ending *this* way to teach us that even when you like to be alone, when your friend checks up on you, it's still nice to spend time together. *Or* another lesson could be that even though lunch was 'spoiled,' being with your friend is more important. So many lessons! What's important, though, is to consider why the author ended it the way that he did."

   You may want to quickly show another example from another text that you have read aloud. You will want this to be quick and concise and consist mostly of you demonstrating. Then you will want to debrief the teaching by saying, "Did you see how I not only thought about how the stories ended but also about *why* the author ended the story this way. I tried to answer the question, 'What may be the important lesson the author wants me to know?'"

During the active engagement, you may decide to have your students practice in their books first. Have them revisit one of the books that they have already read. You might say to your class, "Look back at one of your books, one that both you and your partner have read. First, name how the book ends. You can open up to the ending and reread the last bit, to help refresh your memory. Then together, think, 'Why did the author end the book *this* way? What lesson does the author want readers to learn?'" Circulate and coach a few partnerships. You might intermittently give some quick voiceovers, such as, "Don't forget—don't just *name* the ending, think about *why* the author ended the story this way. What does the author want you to learn?"

In your link, you may want to reiterate the teaching point and name why thinking about endings is so important. You will also want your students to know that thinking about the ending in these ways helps them think about the *whole* story and what the author may have wanted the reader to think about. In the end, you will want students to start getting ready for reading. You can suggest to them to go back to any of the books in their current series, reread the endings, and think about them *or* they can continue on in their current book and when they get to the ending, do this kind of work there.

You might decide to show and reread the anchor chart, "Series Readers Become Experts on Author's Craft" to your students. Then you may want to add a new bullet to your chart and say, "And, just like we did with Frog and Toad and the book you have in your hands right now, you can *also* try to answer the question, Why did the author end the book *this* way? What lessons am I suppose to learn?"

CONFERRING AND SMALL-GROUP WORK

As you confer and pull small groups, you may want to follow up with a couple of the guided reading groups that you started this week. One of the important things you will want to think about is how to scaffold your students so that they can work with increasing independence toward the next level of text complexity. You may want to have students work with a partner in a new text and "set themselves up" to read the book together. Remind them of all they know about reading the covers (front and back) and picture walking through the text. Then you might say, "You are going to read this book twice. The first time, the *two* of you will help each other with the words to get through the book. Then you will reread it. On the second read, not only will you help each other read the words, but this time you will use the anchor chart, 'Series Readers Become Experts on Author's Craft' to talk about what is happening and what you are learning in the book." Your role is one of coach. You will not only want to coach them in the errors that they make or the things that they talk about, but you will want to coach the partnership to work together and be active word solvers and thinkers of the text. After they have read the book twice, you might say to them, "I am going to leave you now. You all can read your book a third time! This time as you read your book, think about what we studied in the minilesson today, 'Why did the author end it this way? What lessons was the author trying to teach?'" Leave your students so that you may work with other groups and individuals. You may circulate back to this group to check into the conversations at the end of the text.

Mid-Workshop Teaching

During the mid-workshop teaching, you might want to stop your readers in the midst of the workshop and give your class some feedback on their work. You may want to tell your students that not only can they think about what the author wants them to learn at the end of the book, but they can think about this question in other parts and in other books in the series as well. Perhaps you will tell them, "As you read any part in your book, you can think, *Why* did the author, write this part, *this* way? What lessons does the author want me to learn?" You may want to give an example, either from a familiar read-aloud text or from one of the partnerships with whom you conferred shortly beforehand. Remind your students that as they read they should be marking parts to share with their book clubs, not *just* thinking about their endings.

SHARE

For today's share, you may want to help your clubs build more skills at not only speaking but also listening. As your students convene in book clubs, you may have them first share out their discoveries about endings and lessons. You might want to give the listeners some tips for thinking about what other club members present and share. You may say something like, "After your club mate shares thoughts about why the author ended the book a particular way, ask your fellow club member to read and show the evidence. If they have a hard time, help them find it in the book or help them think of a new lesson." You will want to listen in to their club talk and coach students to ask questions that help clarify what one another is saying. After you have coached a couple of clubs, you may help extend the talk and conversation by saying, "If a club mate has suggested a lesson that they think the author is trying to teach, check *all* of your books and think, 'Is this true in the *whole* series?' Open your books to see if you, too, have parts that match your club mates' ideas."

Sharing Opinions with the World   BEND III

Session 13

When Readers Love a Series, They Can't Keep It to Themselves

IN THIS SESSION, you'll teach children that part of the joy of reading is sharing what you read with other people.

GETTING READY

- Share the song "The Magic Penny." If you don't know the song, you can find a recording on YouTube (see Connection).
- Write new lyrics to the song on chart paper and have it on hand to display (see Connection).
- Prepare the beginning of a one-day chart called "How We Can Share and Give Away Books that We Love" (see Active Engagement).
- Ask students to bring a book they have finished to the meeting area for swapping (see Share).

MINILESSON

CONNECTION

Use a song to introduce the joy of sharing your reading with other people.

"When I was your age, the kids in my class and I often sang a song called 'The Magic Penny.' Let me sing it to you":

> Love is something if you give it away,
> Give it away, give it away.
> Love is something if you give it away,
> You end up having more.
>
> It's just like a magic penny
> Hold it tight and you won't have any
> Lend it, spend it, you'll have so many
> They'll roll all over the floor.

"To me, the message of that song—that you need to share your love—is a message that has a lot to do with books as well. When I read a great book, everyone I know hears about that book. I carry it with me all day long and bring it up in conversation all the time. I'll be riding on the bus, the book under my arm, and some stranger says to me, 'How do you like that book?' and pretty soon we're talking about the ending or about a really funny part.

"I'll be eating pizza or drinking coffee, the book on the table, and people walk by me and pause, asking, 'How do you like that book?' and pretty soon we're rereading great parts of the book and talking about them.

"And so I changed the words to that song so that the message really is about books!" I said, clipping the new lyrics to the easel. "Will you sing it with me?"

76   GRADE 2: SERIES BOOK CLUBS

Books are something if you give them away
Give them away, give them away
Books are something if you give them away
You end up reading more!
If you love a book that you've just read
and you can't seem to get it out of your head.
Give it, lend it, recommend it.
Because books are something if you give them away
You end up reading more!

❖ **Name the teaching point.**

"Today I want to teach you that when you love a book, and especially when you love a whole series, you can't keep that love to yourself. You can invent ways to get others to love that book, or that series of books, as you do."

TEACHING

Share ways that children have invented to let readers know about books they love.

"This may help to spark an invention in your mind!

"This one kid I know came up with an idea to make and leave little notes throughout the book that she loved for the next reader. She left notes that said things like, 'Here comes a really important part, pay extra extra attention!' 'Can you believe it? I totally think this is a bad idea, you?' and 'Why do you think the character did this? Write your answer first. Mine is on the back!' Cool right? It's like you could have a conversation with her, without her even being there!

"Another kid came up with the idea that he would write valentines to his friends about books that he thought that they should read. He put in his valentines things like, 'I thought of you when I read this and knew you would love it, too, because Cherry Sue forgives Poppleton, just like you forgave me' and 'I think you would love Horrible Harry books because they are so funny and I know you like to joke around, too. Here are some of the things that Harry does and says that are so funny.' Another cool idea and way to share and give your books away to others. If someone wrote me a customized valentine book recommendation, I would definitely read that series—and probably end up loving it, too.

"Both of these examples are of second graders who invented ways to share and give books to others so that they too can fall in love with the books. Not only did they 'invent' ways to share, but they had to reread and get their ideas organized and together to do so!"

In this lesson you are offering students the opportunity to think about inventing unique (and not so unique) ways to share their discoveries from their series. Most people who consider themselves avid readers talk about the importance of book selection. Often, readers' books come from recommendations made by friends, families, and other respected readers. Book recommendations have a powerful role in your students' reading lives as well. You will want to ensure that you are not the only "book recommender" in the class.

The task of recommending a book creates more confidence, helps readers determine and synthesize the important parts of the text, and share ideas. It also improves their "presentation" skills.

SESSION 13: WHEN READERS LOVE A SERIES, THEY CAN'T KEEP IT TO THEMSELVES

ACTIVE ENGAGEMENT

Ask children to talk with each other about their own ideas for sharing books and then record those ideas on a chart.

"Is this sparking an idea and an invention that you could do to get others to love your series books? Think for a second: What can you imagine making or doing with your books to give to others and make them fall in love with your book? When you have one idea, put one finger up. When you have two ideas, put two fingers up. I am starting to see people with ideas. If you have a third idea, put three fingers up." I gave students a few seconds to think and then I said, "Now share your ideas and inventions with your partner.

"Wow, so creative, so innovative! Here's a chart I started with the ideas I told you about. As we create and invent new ideas, we can add them to the chart."

How We Can Share and Give Away Books We Love:
> We can talk about books.
>
> We can leave notes to the reader.
>
> We can write valentines.

We read through the list. "Now let me share some of the ideas that I heard from you. I heard someone say you can act out your books and bring our characters to life. Yup, that could sell it. Another invention, something that you all know, you could write a nomination for your book or series. Yup, that could get others to love a book. Someone else said that they were going to create a game of questions about their book to see if the next reader can answer all of them!" I added these to the chart. Then, I fielded a few more from the others who I may not have heard.

LINK

Send children off to decide how they will share their books.

"So, readers, before you leave the meeting area, you can make a decision of how you might share or invent a way to share your books in the series. After you decide, you will need to get your books out and begin to reread parts and sections that will help you make your invention better and stronger so that whoever receives it will also love that book and series.

"When you are ready, and you know what you are going to work on, put your thumb on your knee. Use the chart we just made to help you if you are stuck and can't come up with an idea, right now! Any of these ideas would be fun to do and will help others *love* your books."

While students will have to think carefully about how *to share with others, so too must they decide* what *to share. You will then expect students to do some rereading to prepare these gifts for others.*

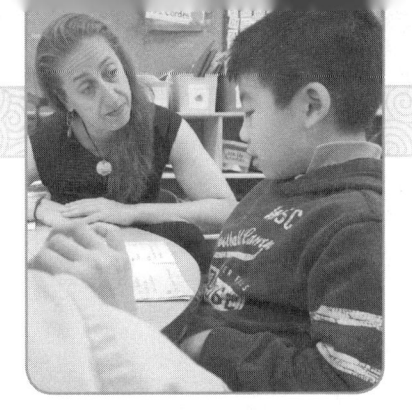

CONFERRING AND SMALL-GROUP WORK

Fostering the Work of the New Bend

THE BEGINNING OF A BEND feels like the natural place to begin a new cycle of small-group work with your students. Before you do, today you may want to not only rally the class's energy to thinking about new ways to share their books but also assess your readers who are reading in the higher bands of text complexity. For example, you will want to motivate and lift the level of your above-benchmark readers who are most likely reading in the level N–Q band of text difficulty. Students who are reading in this band are beginning to read texts with a more complex story structure. The main character may have not just one problem but several. You may want to begin by conferring with several above-benchmark readers today with this lens. As you research your readers today, you may want to examine their Post-its to find evidence of this or you may ask the reader, "Can you tell me about the problems the main character is facing in this series?" or "What is the major problem the character is facing?" You may notice that some children need more explicit instruction on determining importance and and holding on to multiple subplots. Over the next several days, you may decide to support them with a series of strategy groups.

Coach students to find evidence in the book to support what they think makes the book worth sharing.

As students create ways to share, you may discover that some students need help deciding on what to share. Some children may plan to share general information about characters, and you can coach them to determine what is important to share by citing details from the text that show why they love the series. As some of your above-benchmark readers are creating ways to share with their clubs, you might want to suggest that they include how they explored the complex characters in their stories. They might want to create a letter to readers warning them not to get confused or create a game to help readers distinguish the character's major problems from minor ones.

MID-WORKSHOP TEACHING   **Seeking the Best Parts to Share**

"Readers, let me just stop you for a quick second. As you are making things and getting your books ready to share, remember that you will want to show other readers what exactly you loved and why. Use all your knowledge as an expert series reader! For example, you might think about the characters—what makes them special or memorable or funny? You might also think about the author's craft—what kind of literary language did the author use to make the writing extraordinary? Were there parts that painted a vivid picture in your mind? Is there a lesson you want to share from an ending? That is to say, you will need to reread some key parts, to add onto *whatever* it is that you are creating. This will help people see your point of view even better."

As you confer with readers, you may find that many are making "nominations," something that they might have learned during writing workshop. As your students work on their writing, make sure they are reading as well. Look at these nominations to assess the types of examples that they are including. Many times, students either list reasons without supporting them with examples or have a hard time citing an example without copying or summarizing the text. This may be some nice work to do with a student or a small group.

SHARE

Readers Help Each Other with Ideas for Sharing

"READERS, as you work on getting ready to swap your book with a classmate in a couple days, remember that you're not the only one who loves your books as much as you do. You've been working all through this unit with a whole group of series *experts*—your book club! Your club members, who are also thinking about ways to share your series, may have great ideas to add to your project!

"Will you get together with your club right now? Share with the other members of your club what you have done so far. Then, help each other out! Try to think of *other* ideas that colleagues in your club could use to sell the series and help others learn to love the series as much as you do!"

I circulated among the different clubs, listening to them "present" each of their ideas. Before the clubs could say "We're done . . .," I voiced over, "Don't just 'read aloud' the project you made. First, ask for some help. Tell your club to listen for something that might help you make your project even better. You could say, 'See if I need more examples.' or 'Does this part sound convincing enough?'"

Then I went on: "Club members, as you are listening, it's your job to help one another think about how they could make their 'valentine' or 'nomination' even better. Remember, each of you is trying to talk about the *series*, not just one book. So, club members, you can help one another by finding other examples from other books in the series that would be helpful to add to your club members' projects. Okay, back you go, continue sharing and helping one another."

FIG. 13–1 Here a partnership and a book club share their ideas and get ready to make book swaps.

Session 14

Planning the Very Best Way to Share a Book

MINILESSON

CONNECTION

Use a story of how you made a valentine presentation extra special as a model for how children should present their books in an extra special way.

"I remember the very first valentine I made. I made it for my mom. I got all my art supplies out, and I sat at the table to get started. First, I cut a big red paper heart, and then I added lace around the edges. I even sprinkled it with pink glitter.

"And when I thought I was done, I took another look and I realized I could work a bit harder to make it even more special. So, I got back to work. I wrote a poem on the valentine. And I signed my name in fancy letters. I even wrapped it in tissue paper for my mom to open!

"Now, after all the careful work, do you think I just found my mom and tossed the valentine over to her with a shrug and said, 'Here, read this'?" The kids shook their heads no. "Of course not! I wanted it to feel really special. So, I tiptoed into my mom's room and gave her a great, big hug and told her I made a valentine just for her. She was so excited!"

❖ **Name the teaching point.**

"Today I want to teach you that just like you wouldn't carelessly give away a valentine to someone, readers wouldn't carelessly give away a book they love. When you share your love of a book with someone, you do all that you can to make that person feel special by the extra special way you present the book."

IN THIS SESSION, you'll teach children that the best way to share a book or series of books that they love is to prepare a wonderful, thoughtful presentation.

GETTING READY

✔ Consider having children stay at their desks at the beginning of the session so that they are in place to display their book and the work they have begun on how they will present the book (see Connection and Teaching).

✔ Plan to spotlight the different ways students have marked the pages of their books (see Teaching).

TEACHING

Guide the children to notice and learn from the work of their classmates.

"Instead of *me* teaching *you* what you can do to make your invention even more special before you give your book away, I bet you can learn ways to do that from each other. So let's set up a gallery of your inventions, the things you've decided to do with your books to share the love with others.

"Quickly, place your book on your desk and line up by the door. Together, we'll snake walk around the classroom and admire what everyone has done. Pay particular attention to things you notice that you want to try, too. Then, we'll gather together to share those things to make a plan for today's reading work."

I led the class in a single line, snaking around tables and pausing to highlight things I wanted the children to notice. I stopped beside Bailey's desk and held up her book. Fanning through the pages of Post-its, I admired, "Hmm . . . , I notice that this book has lots of Post-its with directions for *how* to act and sound when you read these parts. I think that will help make your reading performance so much stronger when you act it out for others. That might be something some of you add to your books."

I moved on, stopping again at Nathan's desk. I held up his book and noted, "There are *lots* of examples that show *why* this book is so great. Not just one tiny example, but many! I bet some of you will want to add more examples to write nominations." We continued on around the room, naming and noticing things that students had done and that others could replicate.

ACTIVE ENGAGEMENT

Nudge the children toward more ambitious goals by having them talk with one another.

I gathered students back in the meeting area, and once everyone had settled, I continued. "So, right now, make a plan with your partner of what work you'll do today. What might you push yourself to do to present the books you want to share in an even more special way? Turn and talk." I moved around the rug to coach students, nudging them toward more ambitious goals. I prompted them to think, "What *else* can I do? What did I see someone else do, that I can try with my book?

LINK

Send children off to work in preparation for tomorrow's book swap.

"I hear so many grand plans for your reading work! Tomorrow, you'll lend your books to friends in another club. You'll visit them to share these wonderful nominations and valentines and games and performances. The love you have for your book is sure to come pouring right out when you give your book away. So, go back into your books. Look at what you have marked. Are those still the best examples? Reread other parts of the book to see if there are better ones. Go ahead and get working!"

Here you will need to see what students in your class come up with. You should be on the lookout for students who have made Post-its with directions and notes to readers, students who found many examples, and students who gave reasons why others should and will love their series. Point out students whose notes directly address the reader or the audience, who gave little clues in their books, and who made the book seem extra special in any way. You might have readers who did one of these things rather minimally. You will still want to name this to your students: "Look at this!" and then say, "Do it more!"

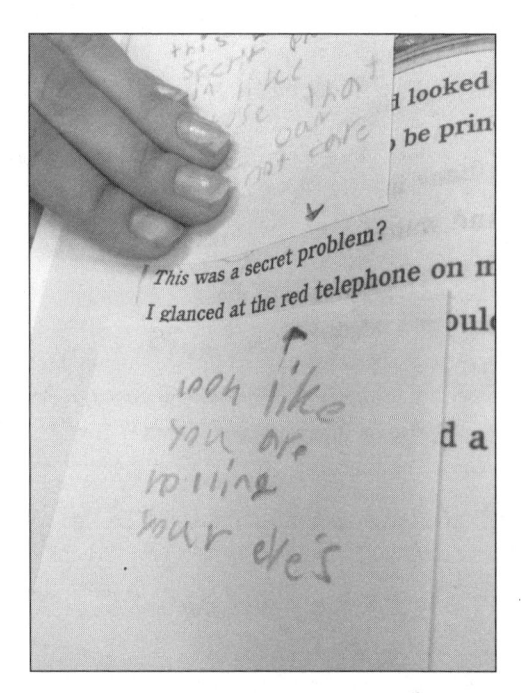

FIG. 14–1 This reader has placed directions in a book to cue expressive voices and dramatic gestures.

CONFERRING AND SMALL-GROUP WORK

Keeping the Work of the Bend Going

TODAY, you may decide to continue the small-group work with several of your above-benchmark readers who are reading in levels N–Q. Based on your conferences, you may determine that you will gather the students to explain that their books not only get longer as they move up levels, they also offer new challenges. One challenge you want them to take on is holding on to the central problem of the story, the one that supports the story's overarching storyline. You can remind students to return to the book blurb on the back of the book for clues to the central problem. You can also ask students to think, "Does this problem thread throughout the story, or does it show one small part of the struggles my character faces?"

During the majority of your strategy lesson, students should be reading independently as you assess and coach the students while they practice the strategy. You may not know the books they are reading, but don't let that intimidate you. Read the blurbs and any Post-its that they have created thus far. You may say, "Show me the work you are doing." Get the child talking, explaining, and working. Try to give the reader little nudges in the right direction. Ask yourself, "Who is doing the work?" Hopefully, you will answer that it is the student!

Continue to support students as they prepare for sharing and giving away the books they love.

After you lead a strategy lesson, you may notice that some students need additional support preparing how they will share their books. You may decide to confer with students, taking on the role of the proficient partner. Your taking on this role will enable the students to practice how they will share with other students. It will help students not only with their speaking skills but also with recognizing parts they need to rethink or revise. You'll want to encourage your readers to spend time going back to reread sections of the text, thinking about what it is they want to share about that part and why they want to share it.

You may also want to direct these children to the anchor charts you used across the first two bends. Encourage students to use these charts as reminders of the types of things they could share in their texts. For example, after rereading the anchor chart from the first bend, a reader may remember a part of the book where a character responded to a problem in an interesting way. Prompt the child to find that part in the book and reread the text carefully, making a plan for the best way to share it. "Remember," you might say, "you can use these charts to help you remember *all* the ways you are an expert in your series books!" Then leave the reader with small versions of the charts to encourage them to replicate this work with another item.

MID-WORKSHOP TEACHING   **Coaching Children to Do More**

"Readers, I am noticing that some of you are getting that, 'I'm done' feeling. If you think you have plenty of examples, reasons, and details that will make your friends love your series, then you can put your book aside. And then you can work on another book to give away! It can be a book from the same series or from another series that you have read. You can do the same kind of invention that you have already done *or* try out a new one. Maybe you will want to do a nomination or put on a play or send a valentine to a friend. You still have several minutes to work and read. Then we will meet in clubs."

SESSION 14: PLANNING THE VERY BEST WAY TO SHARE A BOOK

SHARE

Making Final Preparations for the Book Swap

"READERS, it's time to come to your clubs. Tomorrow is going to be your book swap day! You are going to share and lend your books to others so that they can love your series and become an expert on the series, just like you! As you meet with your club members today, share with everyone what you did to improve the way you are going to present your book. Your club members then can help you figure out if you have enough information and whether it shows your love for the book.

I went to listen and coach a couple of clubs. Many of the clubs needed support with clarifying their ideas. That is, students had great ideas but had difficulty explaining them. I then decided to coach the students to prompt one another to speak more clearly. I said to one club, "As you are listening, to help your club member, try to get her to explain what she means. You could say, 'What do you mean?' or 'Are you saying that . . . ?' This will help your club member present the series in a clear, more powerful way. Try it now. Let's 'rewind' the presentation. Start again. This time, everyone, try to help her clarify her thinking."

"Also, when you do your book swap, you will want to introduce the whole series, so take a moment today to talk with your club members about the most fun, most interesting, or most important thing about your series. What will someone need to know before they dive in? Work together to make these moments count. Put care and thought into your conversation to help you get ready to share your love of the book and series in a way that is extra special."

FIG. 14–2 This partnership is rehearsing before they swap books with another club.

Session 15

Readers Share Books They Love with Friends
A Book Swap

MINILESSON

In the connection, you'll want to create a drumroll for the celebratory feel of today's session. Children will give away one of their cherished books to a classmate in another book club. You might say, "I just love *giving* my friends and family presents—maybe even more than I love *receiving* presents. You might be thinking, Are you serious? You like *giving* presents more than getting them?' But it's true! When you see the smiling face of someone you just gave a special gift to, it makes that love in your heart practically *double* in size! And today, you'll share the love you have for books by gifting them to a friend."

Then, name the teaching point by saying, "Today I want to teach you that when you give a gift, you explain what it is or how it's special or how it works. Readers do the same thing when they share books. They tell the important things to know."

In your teaching, you'll want to demonstrate giving a book introduction that highlights the important details about the whole series, such as the things readers have learned about the main character or the ways the books tend to go. For example, you might introduce Frog and Toad by saying, "In this series, there are two best friends, Frog and Toad. The thing you need to know about Toad is he's usually in a bad mood. But luckily, he has Frog to cheer him up. Frog is really patient and always knows how to make Toad feel better. The way these books go is that each chapter tells its own little story about these two friends. There's usually a problem in the story, but don't worry, they find a way to solve it by the end."

You'll want to name out the moves you made to structure your book introduction. For example, you might say, "Did you notice how I described the two main characters and what I know about how they usually feel or behave? I also included how the books usually go. You might talk a little bit about the way your series books start and end."

During your active engagement, you might say, "Okay, series experts, since you've learned so much about the characters in your books, and the author's craft, show off how much you know. Right now, work with your club to decide on the *most* important things other readers need to know about your series.

"Then, in a few minutes, you'll introduce not only your character but your *whole* series to another club! So discuss what kinds of information you'll want to include. You'll probably want to introduce the characters and explain what's the same in nearly every book. You can describe the relationships the main character has, and you might even read a page out loud to give an example of the precise words the author uses to describe these things. Ready, experts? Start planning your *series* introductions!"

Once students have figured out what to say to introduce the series, they will present a book along with their inventions for sharing the text. You might say something like, "After you introduce your series, the big moment will arrive! That's when you get to give away the book you love in the wonderful, thoughtful way you have prepared! Remember that the way you give away your book is as special as the book itself."

During the link, ask each club to sit side by side with another club. You'll want to pair clubs that are at similar reading levels so that the books they swap will match their just-right reading level. You might say, "The Pinky and Rex club will sit beside the Cam Jansen club. And The Magic Tree House club, will you sit beside the Junie B. Jones club?" Set students up to swap a book with a classmate from a neighboring book club. In effect, children in each club will swap their series.

CONFERRING AND SMALL-GROUP WORK

As you confer and pull small groups, circulate among your readers while they share their books with each other and coach them in doing this work. Take a few moments to listen in to each partnership and then gently raise the level of their work by whispering prompts into the conversation. If you know several students will need a higher level of support with this work, you may pull a small group or partnership to first practice rehearsing their series introductions. You could ask Partner 1 to give a series introduction while you and Partner 2 listen and note specifically what is working especially well and what might be made even better. Then, repeat with Partner 2, keeping in mind all of what was said by Partner 1. When students later move on to reading their new books, you may want to revisit previous small groups to coach readers to greater independence.

Mid-Workshop Teaching

For the mid-workshop teaching, you will want to transition students into reading their new books for the remainder of the independent reading time. You may want to say to them, "As you start reading your new series, be on the lookout not *just* for the things that your friends told you about but also for *other* things that you like and find interesting as well! Remember, now you too can become an expert in this new series!"

SHARE

During today's share, you might say to your students, "Readers, let's get back together with the person who gave you the book you started today. You might want to share what you have read so far, read a little bit and then talk about it. Let them know what you think so far. What do you like about the book and the series? *and*, don't forget to say, 'Thank you!'"

Session 16

Sharing Opinions by Debating

MINILESSON

IN THIS SESSION, you'll introduce the concept of a debate as a way to share opinions about a book.

CONNECTION

Challenge your second graders to try something that older kids do—debate their opinions about a book.

"Second graders, I know you all have invented *lots* of ways to share your books to get others to love them! I have *one* more way that I think is really cool. Are you up for it? It's something that fifth-graders do when they read. Do you want me to tell you? After they read, to share about their books, sometimes they *debate*! They ask a question, one that could have two answers, and then some readers take one side and argue for it and some readers take another side argue for it—they debate! Do you want to try? Are you up to doing what fifth-graders do? Let's do it. Let's have a debate!"

GETTING READY

- Be prepared to read a familiar story from a series book. We use "Alone" from *Days with Frog and Toad* by Arnold Lobel (see Teaching and Active Engagement).
- Ensure students have Post-its on hand to mark pages with evidence for their debate (see Mid Workshop Teaching).

❖ **Name the teaching point.**

"Today I want to teach you that readers debate the opinions they have about their books. You can read (and reread) to collect evidence to support your side, or opinion."

TEACHING AND ACTIVE ENGAGEMENT

Assign students to one side of a debate or the other. Ask them to listen to a familiar story to collect evidence that supports their side.

"So, let's have a debate about a book that we know so well, *Days with Frog and Toad*. Let's debate whether or not Frog is a good friend. Some may say he is, but some may say he isn't! In a debate, there are two answers, or sides. For this debate, I am going to tell you which side you are on." Then I motioned with my hands, as if slicing a giant loaf of bread down the middle, dividing the meeting area in two. "All of you on this side of the meeting area will be on the side 'Yes, Frog is a good friend' and everyone on this side of the meeting area will be on the side 'No, he is not a good friend.'

"I'm going to reread the story 'Alone,' and as I read, be on the lookout for examples that fit with your side of the debate. If you hear something that shows Frog being a good friend, make a special note of that. If you hear some things where he *isn't* being a good friend, you will want to remember that. Are you ready?"

I began to read "Alone" out loud. As I read, I frequently paused to voice over things like, "Ooh, does that show him being a good friend? Does this show him *not* being a good friend?" or "Oh, boy, that seems important to remember for a debate about whether Frog is a being a good friend or not" and "Are you finding something here, that goes with your side?" When I finished with the story, I turned to the "friend" side partnerships and said, "Now, turn and talk to your partner about *all* the ways that Frog is a good friend, and," I continued, talking to the "not friend" side partnerships, "all the ways that Frog is *not* a good friend. Everyone, try to use as many examples as you remember from the story."

Direct the students on how to begin and hold their debate.

"Now, let's start the arguing—the *debate*! Line up and face someone on the other side. Shake hands. To start, you are going to say, 'I take the position that Frog *is* a good friend.' Then you are going to say your reasons and examples. Then your counterpart, your partner, will say, 'I take the position that Frog is *not* a good friend.' Then *you* will list your reasons and as many examples as you can. Are you ready to argue? To *debate*? Go!"

LINK

Prepare students for the next debate.

"Readers, congratulations on your debate! First one! Don't worry if you wanted to debate the other side instead. You can do that at recess!" I winked and smiled at the class. "When you debate, you have to get ready by collecting lots of reasons and examples to support your side. That makes your debate stronger!"

"Today, as you go off to read in your series, you are all going to get ready for another debate, which you will have tomorrow in class. You are all going to debate this question: Is the main character of your series a good friend or not? Your club will argue both sides: two of you will argue yes, and two will argue no. Before you start reading, decide who will take which side. If you need me to, I can assign you!"

This is a bit different from the typical minilesson. In this session, you are combining your teach and your active engagement as you walk your students through the process of holding a debate.

The debate that I chose here, "Is Frog a good friend or not?," was purposefully one that could be applied to many of the series books that your students are reading. The idea in this work is not to develop a fancy thesis, but rather to be able to take a position (either side) and use evidence from multiple texts to support the opinion. Students will have lots of fun with debate. Make sure that they learn how to debate in respectful ways and use as much text evidence as possible so that their arguments are grounded in what they have read.

CONFERRING AND SMALL-GROUP WORK

Setting Students Up to Work Independently

AS YOU WORK WITH STUDENTS TODAY, you may decide to pull several small groups. You may first pull your above-benchmark readers to continue the cycle of small-group work you started earlier in the bend. This time, you may start by asking students to share the work they have been doing around studying characters and navigating more complex plotlines. You may also ask students to interpret the work they are doing around characters to prepare for their debate.

Pull together students who need your help finding evidence to support their argument.

You may notice that several students need additional support to reread with this lens in preparation for their debate. Pull these students together and quickly demonstrate how you would reread a section of text to make an argument for whether the main character is acting like a good friend. After a quick demonstration, encourage students to begin practicing this work as they reread their independent books. Coach each student individually in the small groups. For example, after noticing a character's actions or words, you'll want the reader to consider *why* a character is responding in this way. Then prompt the student to think about what this tells us about whether or not the character is a good friend. Encourage readers to use Post-its to jot down places where they find evidence to support their claim.

Confer with students who struggle with determining importance.

Before you pull your next small group or conduct one-on-one conferences, you may need to take the pulse of the class. As you circulate around the classroom, you may notice that several students have many Post-its in their books. Placing too many Post-its may not only slow down the students' reading, it may also show that the students are struggling with determining importance. As you investigate the students' jots, teach students to choose the jots that are most important and will help support the argument. It's possible that the jots seem inaccurate or insignificant. Sharing mentor Post-its with students will give them examples of the type of work that is helpful.

MID-WORKSHOP TEACHING
Collecting Evidence from the Text

"Readers, you need to collect evidence for your side. As you read, you might say to yourself, 'I can't say that Poppleton is being a good friend here where he sprays Cherry Sue with a hose. That's mean.' *But* as a debater, you can turn on your super debating thinking brain and say to yourself, 'Is there *anything* thing here that *could* show he is being a good friend?'

"Like, I could say, 'Poppleton feels so badly about losing his cool. It's not that he *doesn't* want to be her friend. He just got frustrated, and even friends make mistakes! Good friends make mistakes, *but* they always apologize.' See how I am trying to get that to be on my side? As you read, collect more examples.

"You might go back to some parts in your books that you didn't think could be an example, and if you push your debating brain a little more, you might be able to use that example, too! Don't forget to mark your pages with Post-its to help you keep track of your evidence."

SHARE

Working Together to Strengthen Arguments

"READERS, today is not the debate. Tomorrow is. So, get together with your partner in your club who is on your *same* side. Share with one another all the parts and examples that you found to go with your side of the debate. Get ready for arguing tomorrow. You will want to do three things: one, make sure the examples *show* your side. Two, help each other say why and how it fits with your side. Three, help each other find more examples. Go ahead, meet together, and get ready! Make your arguments the strongest that they can be!"

As I went around to coach and teach the different partnerships, I gave them quick tips and then voiced over to the whole class, sharing the tip with everyone. The first tip I shared was, "Partners, as you are trying to figure out if the example matches your side, reread! This will help you make a decision!" Then I found some partnerships just sharing examples and forgetting to explain why, so I voiced over to everyone, "After your partner shares the example either ask them, 'How does that fit with our side?' or say, 'That fits with our position because . . .'. Try it!"

Some of your students may be quite good at sharing examples and saying how they fit with their position. I decided to challenge a couple of partnerships. I brought two partnerships together and said to them, "I see that you all have lots of examples. To get ready for tomorrow, you can begin to think, 'What if the other side says . . .'. By thinking about what your opponents might say, you can plan what you might say back to them. The two of you can have a practice round, before tomorrow. This will also get you ready. Try it!"

Make Your Arguments Even Stronger!

1. Make sure the examples *show* your side.

2. Help each other say WHY and how it fits with your side.

3. Help each other find more examples.

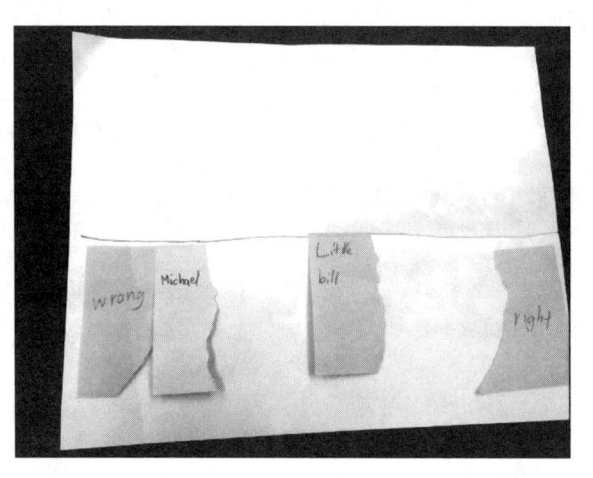

FIG. 16–1   A partnership made this scale to help debate their opinions about Little Bill and Michael in *The Meanest Thing to Say*. The club debated which character was more right and whether Little Bill is usually right or wrong across the series.

Session 17

Celebration: Supporting Reasons with Examples to Strengthen Debate Work

MINILESSON

In your connection, you may decide to celebrate the growth your readers have made across this unit and across the year. You might quickly call a few students up to the front of the room and have them stand beside a meter stick, marveling at how they've grown so much, just like Jack's fairy tale beanstalk. You might say, "I remember on the very first day of second grade, when you walked into this classroom. You knew a lot about reading then, but you know even *more* now! You've grown not just taller, you've grown wiser." Then, go on to say that today you'll celebrate this final unit with mini-debates. Each club will host a debate and it will be important to prepare to make those debates even stronger.

Then, name the teaching point. Say, "Today I want to teach you that to make your debate stronger, it's important to be able to say more about your reasons. You can use the book to give examples and say, 'In the book, . . .' or 'For example, ...'"

As you teach, you'll probably want to go back to the Frog and Toad debate you began during yesterday's lesson. You might say, "Watch how I use the book to say more about the reasons I think Frog is a good friend. Ready? I think Frog is a good friend because he tries to help Toad. Hmm, now I need to say more. *How* does he help Toad?" You'll want to think aloud and flip through the pages to find an example as a way of making this process replicable. "Oh, yes! I think Frog is a good friend because he tries to help Toad. *For example*, Frog points out all the things that need to be cleaned up, like the dishes in the sink. *In the book*, it says, 'Your kitchen sink is filled with dirty dishes,' said Frog."

Then, rename your process, highlighting how you gave a reason and then used the details from the book to give an example.

During the active engagement, nudge kids to think about their side of the debate, from yesterday's lesson. "Partners who are on the side that believes their main character is a good friend, say *why*. Then, think about examples that show *how* the character is a good friend. *What* does the character do or say? Remember, use the words *for example* or *in the book* to help you say more about your reasons." Coach the other half of the class to do the same to debate that their main character is not a good friend. Then, prompt partners to turn and debate, giving their reason and supporting it with examples.

Link today's lesson by explaining that this is a strategy students can use whenever they are debating or writing about their opinions. You may suggest that as kids reread today, they use a Post-it to mark examples that support their position so that they can easily reference evidence from the text during their debate.

CONFERRING AND SMALL-GROUP WORK

As you confer and pull small groups, consider pulling a group of readers together to practice the debating they'll do during the share. You might teach the readers to predict what their classmates on the other side might plan to say in support of their opinion and show the readers how to think through and plan to "talk back" to the other side's examples. After meeting with one group, quickly switch to another and do the same sort of work to ensure a lively debate when the time comes at the end of the session.

Mid-Workshop Teaching

During this time, suggest that partnerships caucus, meeting together quickly to share the examples they've found to support their side of the debate. Encourage children to reread and mark these pages. Then, prompt children to read on to find more examples to make their opinions even more compelling.

SHARE

For today's share, you'll host your unit celebration with club debates. You may choose to invite other teachers or the school principal or families to join the celebration. If so, you'll want to divide the visitors among the small groups so that each club has an audience. Remind the kids that they have truly become experts in their series books. They can use all that they know about their series books and the characters to give reasons *and* examples to talk back and forth. You may also want to remind children that debates are a way to disagree politely and to use manners when taking turns and talking back. You'll likely circulate around the room, facilitating these mini-debates and coaching in to support the students, as needed.

You might nudge the children to think about a way to end their debate, perhaps coming to a consensus, restating their position, or shaking hands. You might say, "Just like books have endings and units have endings, talks should have endings, too. Decide together on a way to bring your debate to a close. You might take turns repeating your opinion. You might list back your reasons. You may even shake hands!"

Read-Aloud and Shared Reading

Read-Aloud

GETTING READY

✓ Choose a chapter book or a collection of short stories with an engaging storyline, interesting characters, and rich language. We use *The Stories Julian Tells* by Ann Cameron.

✓ Ask students to bring a clipboard, several Post-its, and a pencil to the meeting area.

✓ Prepare a blank piece of chart paper or create large Post-its to model jotting during the read-aloud.

✓ Use a document camera to display portions of the text when you would like the students to use text evidence.

✓ Prepare another piece of chart paper or prepare your white board to be ready to list the rules of accountable talk.

✓ Display the accountable talk chart from the first unit of study, "Readers Talk about Books," so that it is ready to refer to.

✓ Insert the Post-it notes for the corresponding day into your copy of *The Stories Julian Tells*.

Getting Ready: BOOK SELECTION

In keeping with the work of this unit, you will want to choose a variety of stories to read to your students that are part of a series. You will want to choose a variety of books that match a few different levels to read aloud to your students. We selected the Julian series because the stories are engaging and relatable to second-graders. The chapters are short stories, you can teach students about finding similarities and differences in the author's work and in the characters quite easily. This is to say, some of the read-alouds in a series should be short stories, while others should be one continuous chapter book. We also selected Julian, because it is a text level N, which is just above the end-of-the-year expectation for second-graders, supporting readers with the demands of more complex texts.

Another consideration for choosing this book and series was to find a text that could serve as a model for studying craft and figurative language. This text, particularly, uses literary language and devices in ways that enhance the reader's understanding about the character and the story.

Here, we have outlined a plan for the first few days of read-aloud work with the first three stories in the book. You will then want to use the template, the same types of questions and skills, to complete the entire book. You may decide to revisit a short story or an excerpt of a short story to use not only in your mini-lessons but also with your class and/or small groups during shared reading.

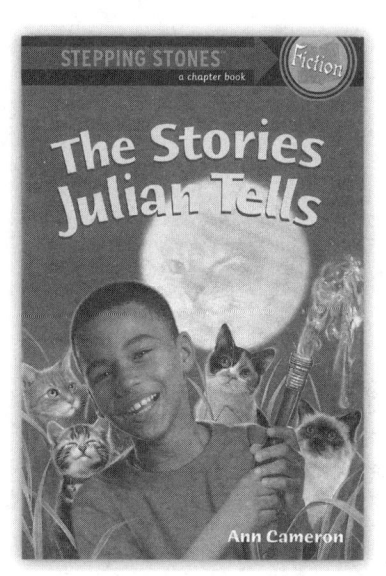

The Stories Julian Tells by Ann Cameron. Illustrated by Ann Strugnell.

SESSIONS 1 and 2

BEFORE YOU READ

Model how you take a sneak peek—previewing a text by reading the title, studying the cover, and reading the back blurb.

You will want to start off your read-aloud by explaining to students what series you have chosen and how they are going to be reading and collecting information about characters in the series. You might start off by saying something like, "Readers, to start off our new unit on series book clubs, I thought we could read a few short stories in a series about a character named Julian. The first book is called *The Stories Julian Tells*. We are going to read a few short stories that 'Julian tells' and become a real expert on this series. Let's start to collect some information, knowledge, and ideas about the characters who star in this series. Let's preview and do a sneak peek to see what we can learn about them from the front and back covers and the table of contents before we begin reading."

Unpack figurative language from the title of the first chapter to predict what it could be about.

Then, you will want to focus on using the chapter title to anticipate what the first chapter might be about. You may say to the students, "Let's look at the first chapter title. It is titled, 'The Pudding Like a Night on the Sea.' Wow, that sounds like some fancy language! You know that when you see similes it is your job to compare two things and think about how they are connected. What are you thinking? How is pudding connected to a night on the sea? Turn and discuss it with your partner." As you coach partnerships, you may help students see that a night on the sea can be something pleasurable and desirable.

Prepare readers to collect as much information as possible about the characters in the story.

This story is written in first person, and readers may need support keeping tracking of characters. For example, you might let children know that when they hear the words *I* or *me* in the story, they usually refer to Julian. Also, the description of the characters comes from Julian's perspective, and that may be need to be explored. Before reading you may want to say, "As we begin reading the first chapter today, I want you to learn as much as you can about the characters in the story: Julian, his brother Huey, and their father. Julian is the narrator. He is telling the story."

AS YOU READ

Page 2: Pause and prompt students to use details from the text to describe Julian's father. Then, model creating a mentor Post-it about Julian's father.

In the first few pages of this text, we learn about Julian's father and Julian's perception of him. The text describes how Julian's father decides to make pudding for his wife, and the author uses descriptive language to describe him. You may say, "We just learned so much about Julian's father. Turn and discuss him with your partner." After the students turn and

---

SESSION 1: AS YOU READ

p. 2: Pause and prompt students to use details from the text to describe the characters.

"We just learned a lot of information about the characters. Let's collect some thoughts about what we now know about them and how they are acting/behaving."

talk, you may decide to voice over, sharing a few examples of things you overhear. You may say, "I heard some of you say that Julian's father is thoughtful and kind because he wants to make a pudding for his wife. I also heard some of you say that Julian's father can get really excited because he laughs so loudly that the windows shake, and when he is mad, Julian shakes." Then, you may create a mentor Post-it for Julian's father, displaying the key information collected about him.

Page 5: Pause and prompt students to continue gathering information about the characters in the text.

After the next few pages, you may decide to pause and ask students, "Before we read on, let's make sure we are holding on to the story and keeping all of the characters straight. Think about what has happened so far and stop and jot important information you are learning about Huey and Julian. Who are they? What are they doing? How are they acting?" After the students have a few moments to jot, ask partners to share their ideas with each other.

Page 6: Pause and prompt students to predict what will happen next.

As you read this page, you may want to use your voice to clearly stress how the dad tells the boys to leave the pudding alone. Then, you may say, "Hmm . . ., the father just told the boys to leave the pudding alone. What do you know about the boys so far? What problem could arise here? Turn and talk to your partner about what is going to happen next in the story!" As students turn and talk, coach readers beyond one- or two-word answers to explain how the story might unfold.

Page 8: Pause and prompt students to confirm and/or revise their predictions. Then, ask students to add more to their jots about the characters.

Encouraging readers to check in on their predictions is important. We want readers to either confirm or revise their predictions because this action supports monitoring for meaning. Chances are that most children predicted that Julian and Huey would eat the pudding. You may say, "Wow, that was a powerful scene! What did you learn about the characters in this scene? Turn and talk to your partner about what ideas you're having now." Then, after a few moments, you may ask students to add more about Julian and Huey to their stop-and-jots.

Page 12: Pause and prompt students to describe the characters' feelings, citing examples from the text. Then, ask the students to predict how the story will end.

This is another powerful scene where the characters really show how they are feeling, both through their actions and their words. You may ask students, "Pick a character to tell your partner about. Describe how the character is feeling and tell what part in the text lets you know that. Turn

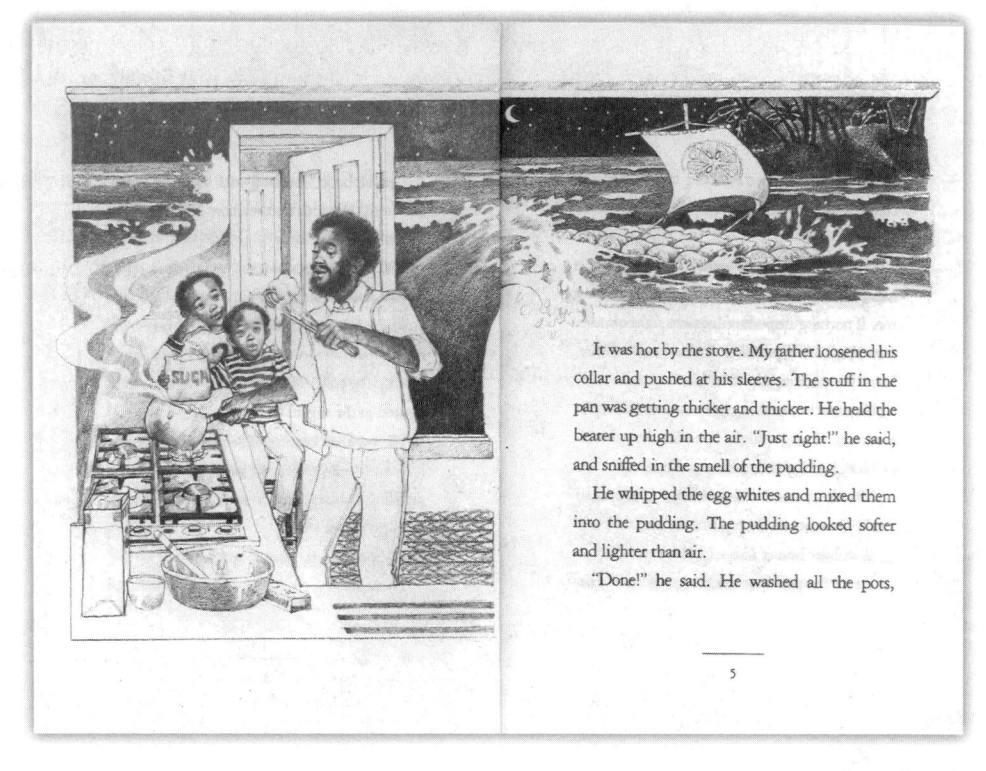

READ-ALOUD

and talk to your partner." Then, you may place a few key pages under the document camera for the children to reference to cite text examples from the text.

Before reading the end of the chapter, you may ask students to predict how the chapter might end. You might reread, "'I can tell you one thing,' he said. 'There is going to be some beating here now! There is going to be some whipping!'" Then you might ask, "How do you think the story will end? What makes you think so? Turn and talk to your partners."

Page 16: Stop at the end of the chapter for students to confirm and revise their predictions and to discuss how the problem was solved.

The story may confuse some readers, and it is important that students are monitoring and discussing the story. You may ask children to discuss how the problem was solved. You might ask, "Did the story end the way that you anticipated, or was it a surprise?" After a few moments, you may want to highlight what a few children discussed.

AFTER YOU READ

Review whole-class discussion routines and prompt children to make their book talk stronger.

After a powerful chapter, you may want to give children time to think deeply and discuss the text with other students. Discussing interpretations of a text deepens comprehension and allows readers to see the text in new ways. It also helps to scaffold the work readers will be doing as they talk across texts in series book clubs.

You might, on this first day, engage the kids in a whole-class discussion. You might say, "We are going to have a book talk. You are becoming expert book talkers. What kinds of things do you do to have a *strong* book talk? Teach me!" You may choose to create a quick list as children offer suggestions. For example, you might say, "These are wonderful things you should do *every* time you talk about books":

- Listen and *add* on.
- Ask questions.
- Use examples from the book.

"Let's talk about the first chapter of *The Stories Julian Tells*. Many of us were surprised how the characters behaved in the story. Some of us couldn't believe that the boys ate the pudding after their dad told them not to. Others thought that their dad was really going to whip or beat the boys because he was so mad. So, let's think a bit more about this. Let's think about the problem in this story. What do you think about how the characters—the dad, the mom, Julian, Huey—handled the situation? Think about this for a moment and use your stop-and-jots to get your ideas ready to share.

"When you are having a book talk, you can refer to the 'Readers Talk about Books' chart to keep the conversation going."

To facilitate the book talk, you might have students sit in a circle so that they can see each other. Once they get started talking, let them take over leadership of the discussion, deciding what to say and who should talk next. Keep a low profile, offering prompts only when the discussion needs to be nudged back on track or restarted after a lull. You might begin by asking, "Who would like to start today's discussion?"

SESSIONS 3 and 4

BEFORE YOU READ

Prompt students to review their notes about characters and discuss what they have learned so far.

As students begin to read more complex chapter books, they will find that the books may be either cumulative or episodic in structure. This story follows the latter structure, enabling readers to read isolated adventures of the characters. As you read the next chapter of *The Stories Julian Tells* by Ann Cameron, you may want to prompt students to use what they already know about the characters to help predict how they might act in a new episode. You may say, "Readers, pull out your notes about Julian, Huey, and their father. Take a second to reread them to get your mind back to the story. Talk to your partner about what we know about the characters." As the students look back at their Post-its, you may place your mentor Post-its on the easel for the students to see.

Coach students to use the chapter title and study the illustrations to predict what the chapter will be about.

Before you read aloud the next chapter, you may want to begin by reading aloud the chapter title to predict what the chapter will be about. You may say, "The next chapter is titled, 'Catalog Cats.' What do you think that could possibly mean? Quick, turn and share your predictions with your partner!" Children will probably say that there are cats and a catalog in the chapter because they most likely will not have enough information to predict the problem of the story. Thus, the turn-and-talk should be very brief.

Acknowledge that the title doesn't give a lot of information for predicting what the chapter will be about, so you'll want to nudge kids to search for meaning using the illustrations. Place page 20 under the document camera and ask students to study the illustration to see if it gives them additional clues. After the children turn and talk, recap what the children say. Many children may say that it looks like one of the boys is dreaming about cats, or that the cats seem like magic cats. Then you may say, "Let's look at the next illustration to see if it will help us gather more information about the chapter." Then, preview the illustrations on pages 25 and 26. The students will quickly notice that there are cats all over the house. Then, ask a couple of volunteers to summarize all that they have learned about the chapter from the title and the illustrations: Huey is upset and crying. Father looks like he is hugging Huey, and Julian looks bored or feels bad about something.

Then, voice back students' predictions, "Many of you think that Huey was dreaming about cats and that he is upset or scared about something. Some of you think that Julian is part of the problem. Okay, let's read to find out!"

AS YOU READ

Page 19: Coach and prompt students to revise and/or confirm predictions. Then, coach students to connect information about characters across chapters.

Stopping at this part of the text will enable readers to monitor for meaning and revise their predictions. Many children will likely have predicted that Huey was upset or mad about something. Now, students will be able to begin to fill in the blanks identifying the problem of the story. You may say, "It looks like you are learning about how these catalog cats fit into the story. What is happening so far? What are you realizing about the story now?" After students turn and talk, summarize what the students discussed.

Then, you may prompt students to think a bit more deeply about Julian. You may ask students to look back at their notes about Julian and think about, "How does the information from this chapter fit with what we already know about him? Did we learn anything new about him?" After a few moments, the students may begin to turn and talk to their partners. You may want to summarize their conversations stating that in both chapters Julian does tell a lie, although in this chapter his lie is kind of mean to his little brother. The author is revealing that Julian can be hurtful and not very nice."

Page 23: After reading the first sentence, prompt and coach students to think inferentially about the characters' actions.

As children are reading texts of increasing complexity, they may need to study what the thoughts and actions of the character say about him or her. After reading the first sentence on page 23, you may nudge kids to consider the character's feelings. Say, "I wonder why Julian was thinking about going somewhere else. How do you think he is feeling?" With prompting, most students will be able to discuss this with ease; however, without prompting, they may not pause to consider details such as what the character is thinking.

Page 24: Coach and prompt students to use prior knowledge about the characters to predict how they might handle the problem.

At the end of page 24, you may stop to help children use all that they know about Julian and his father to predict how they will handle the problem. You may want to encourage students to think back to the first chapter to think about how Julian his father acted when the problem occurred. You may ask the students, "Based on what we know about Julian and his father, how do you think that the characters will react to *this* situation?" Then, you may place the illustration on the document camera to remind the students of the scene.

SESSION 2: AS YOU READ

p. 19: Then, coach students to connect information about characters across chapters.

"How does the information from this chapter fit with what we already know about the character? Did we learn anything new about the character?"

After the students make predictions, you may highlight that many students said that Julian's father is not going to act in a predictable way. Some children think that he is going to try to teach Julian a lesson, like in the first chapter. Whatever the students say, look for evidence that they are carrying information about the characters from one chapter to the next.

Page 28: Prompt students to revise and/or confirm predictions. Then, ask the students to infer why they think the character acted in a certain way.

You may ask students to retell the scene as you listen in to check for comprehension. The father's reaction to Julian and Huey may confuse some students. Chances are they predicted that Julian was going to have to repent for his lie in some way; many children will not guess that the father continues the lie for Huey's benefit.

After the students retell, you may ask the students to revise their predictions, imagining how the new information may support the ending of the chapter. You may also ask students to think about why the boys' father may have continued Julian's lie. For example, you might help kids to understand that he was trying to console Huey in a gentle way. This concept may need to be explored with the students because it may not make sense to students who think more literally.

Page 30: Ask students to summarize the key events of the story to partners.

As students continue to read more and more complex texts, they will need to practice determining importance and summarizing the key details of the story. After you finish the chapter, you may ask students to think about the chapter and practice summarizing the chapter with partners. You may ask partners to listen carefully and ask questions if important information is missing.

AFTER YOU READ

Encourage students to compare and contrast the characters' actions and behaviors across both chapters.

After reading two chapters of the story, you may want to give the class additional practice talking across both stories. You may give partners the opportunity to first explore the question, "What are we learning about the characters across both stories? How are the characters' actions and feelings similar? How are they different?" After you give partners time to explore their ideas, you may decide to open up a whole-class conversation.

After the students form a circle in the meeting area, quickly remind students of the rules for whole-class conversation and reference the accountable talk chart. As students begin their conversation, you may want to circulate around the outside of the circle, coaching students only as needed.

SESSION 5

BEFORE YOU READ

Prompt students to recap what they learned about the characters in the first two chapters. Then, show students how to use the chapter title to predict what the next chapter will be about.

The first two chapters of *The Stories Julian Tells* by Ann Cameron are episodic, but the third chapter builds upon the second. You may decide to begin your read-aloud today by asking students to talk to their partners about all that they have learned about the characters so far.

After the students recap the story, read the chapter title to them. You may say, "The next chapter is called 'Our Garden.' This chapter continues the story of the catalog cats. Let's look to see if there are any illustrations to help us predict what might happen." Then, place the text under the document camera, flipping through the first few pages, stopping on page 35. "Yeah, you noticed it, too!" I said as I pointed to the cats. "Are you thinking that in this chapter they plant the seeds and grow the garden? Are you also thinking that the catalog cats will be mentioned?"

AS YOU READ

Page 34: Pause and prompt students to continue to examine characters to infer and grow a deeper understanding about them.

As you read the third chapter, your students will see yet another side of Julian. "Thumbs up if you are noticing ways that Julian's behavior has changed. Turn and share what you're noticing with your partner." You could place the part of the text where Julian works in the garden under the document camera so that students can reference it as they discuss with partners.

Then, ask students to think closely about Julian's actions to think about what new information they could add to their Post-its. "What words might you use to describe him? Add to your stop and jots." As children add to their stop-and-jots, you may notice that they are adding words like *hardworking* or *determined*.

Page 36: Reread and examine parts of the text to examine how the character has changed.

At the end of the chapter, we see that Julian has grown or matured. At the beginning of Chapter 2, he got excited to tease and lie to his brother. At the end of Chapter 3, we see that Julian was happy that Huey's garden vegetables were

READ-ALOUD

101

even more plentiful than his own. He was happy for his brother's success. You may decide to reread the last paragraph of the chapter, asking students to think about how Julian has changed from the beginning of the story to the end.

AFTER YOU READ

Encourage students to generate topics for the whole-class conversation.

As students become more equipped at talking about texts and growing ideas, you will want to release the scaffold to enable them to decide on the questions they would like to explore around the text. You may say, "Instead of giving you the questions to talk about, I think you're ready to do that work on your own today. What do you think would make a great whole-class conversation? Turn and talk to your partner. What might we discuss today?" Students may choose to talk about particular characters, such as the dad or Julian. They may choose topics like parenting or helping others. Or students may raise questions that begin, "why did . . .?" or "what did you think when . . .?" You will want to listen in and coach students as they talk with their partners encouraging students to name questions that are large enough to create a strong conversation.

After discussing possibilities, choose one that you think would lead to strong talk. You may decide to talk about how the family shows love for each other in this story and what readers can learn from it. You may decide to talk about the lessons that Julian learns. Whichever you choose, you will want the students to be passionate about the conversation.

SESSION 3: AFTER YOU READ

End: Encourage students to generate topics for a whole-class conversation.

"What do you think would make a great whole-class conversation? Turn and talk to your partner. What might we discuss today?"

Shared Reading

Text Selections

› *The Stories Julian Tells* by Ann Cameron.

› Song of your choice, for example "Magic Penny" by Malvina Reynolds.

We have selected, "My Very Strange Teeth," which is a short story from Ann Cameron's *The Stories Julian Tells*. This particular story is one that emphasizes the relationship between Julian and his dad and is filled with emotion. Typically, most of your students are learning how to read texts that have quite a bit of dialogue and few pictures. This story exemplifies these qualities and will be a good practice text for them. We also chose this text because it is above the end-of-the-year benchmark level. It is a level N text, which will give students the experience of reading a complex text with scaffolded support.

DAY ONE: Warm Up, Book Introduction, and First Read

On this day, you'll want to both revisit a familiar text, like a song, poem, or even another excerpt from a text you have read earlier this year, and introduce the text that you will be reading across the next five days. The nature of the shared reading lessons, focusing on specific elements of the text or skills of the readers, assumes that students are already familiar with the text. You may decide to choose an excerpt from a read-aloud or picture book that you have already read. We have selected "My Very Strange Teeth," which is a short story from Ann Cameron's series, *The Stories Julian Tells*. During this first read, you will want to focus on and support understanding the story and thinking about what is happening.

You will also want to be sure that you read with a fluent voice, sweeping your eyes across each line to read in mostly three- to four-word chunks. You may find that students' voices lag behind or peter off at certain points. Do not worry. Keep your voice fluent and use intonation. In the moment, reread certain lines or paragraphs to pick up more voices along the first read.

Since your students haven't read this text themselves before, you still may want to practice using all three sources of information—meaning, syntax, and visual cues (MSV)—as you read to tackle words. You may wish to select a couple of words to mask with Post-its so that *all* students work on first using meaning to solve words. You may also choose a couple of words because they are extra long, are new vocabulary, or have some feature of phonics that you are studying in word study, such as plurals or diphthongs, or vocabulary work including prefixes and suffixes or homophones.

WARM UP: "Magic Penny" by Malvina Reynolds

Quickly read an accessible or familiar text to build confidence, excitement, and fluency.

Choose a song or a poem that you'll reread across the week to warm up students' reading (and singing) voices. We suggest "Magic Penny" because it shares a sweet sentiment about love and kindness. It is also referenced at the start of Bend III, when students are taught a version of the song with new lyrics, but if children are not yet familiar with it, you can find a recording on YouTube. Whatever text you choose, invite kids to join in a choral read to prepare for the day's shared reading work.

BOOK INTRODUCTION AND FIRST READING: "My Very Strange Teeth" from *The Stories Julian Tells* by Ann Cameron

Set students up to begin the work of the shared reading text.

You will want to set your students up to reread a short excerpt from the story "My Very Strange Teeth." You may want to say to them, "I thought we would all revisit and reread a part from the story 'My Very Strange Teeth' together.

DAY ONE FOCUS

✓ Reading for comprehension—clarifying unknown vocabulary and phrases

✓ Using sources of information (MSV) to figure out tricky words

GETTING READY

✓ Prepare a copy of a song or poem to sing with students. We suggest "Magic Penny" by Malvina Reynolds. Make sure the copy is large enough for all students to read, or be ready to project it (see Warm Up).

✓ Become familiar with a chapter from a familiar text a level or two above the reading level of most of your students in preparation for sharing it with them. Here we suggest an excerpt (pages 48–51) from the short story "My Very Strange Teeth" from the book *The Stories Julian Tells* by Ann Cameron (see Book Introduction and First Reading).

✓ Cover three to five words in the text so that students can apply word-solving strategies (MSV). We suggest *answered*, *thread*, and *doorknob* (see Book Introduction and First Reading).

We all loved that story so much and there were so many parts where we were gasping and oohing and aahing! Does everyone remember the story? Quickly, across your five fingers, retell the most important things that happen in this story. In the beginning Julian wants . . . . Keep going."

Then you will want to introduce the part that they will be rereading together. You may choose a selection from the beginning of the text, such as pages 48 through 51. You choose the length and the part, though here in these pages there is quite a bit of work to be done. You might say to your class, "Do you remember the part at the beginning, when the dad is ready to help pull Julian's tooth out of his mouth, and he comes up with a few ways? Well, I thought we would reread from the bottom of page 47, when the dad is ready to pull out the tooth the first way. Remember, he says, 'You won't feel a thing!' But, does Julian believe that? Nope, he sure doesn't, because he is nervous it will really hurt. Get your voices ready, and let's read."

Select three to five words to cover. Stop to practice using multiple sources of information to figure out and check the word.

You may decide to mask a couple of words on the first read, such as *answered*, *thread*, and *doorknob*. In this text, there are lots of references to the ways that the characters say things, so to decode the word, *answered*, you will want students to think about various possibilities. "What kind of word might fit here? What would make sense and sound right?" Students will be mostly familiar with the dialogue tag, *said*, so follow up by asking, "What letter do you expect to see at the beginning of *said*? Yes, *said* begins with the letter *s*." Reveal just the first letter to see if it is an *s*. Children may be quite surprised to see the letter *a* revealed! Push them to come up with some other words that would make sense here and start with *a*. You might need to point out the question-answer dialogue to help them make meaningful guesses. Again, take guesses for words that make sense and the letters children expect to see, and then check their guesses with the reveal. Always put the words back into context by rereading the sentence smoothly before continuing. As you read on, repeat the same kind of prompting with any other words that you select. Remind students to draw on all their sources for word solving, including the anchor chart from Unit 1, "When Words Are Tricky, Roll Up Your Sleeves!"

SHARED READING

> **ANCHOR CHART**
>
> ### When Words Are Tricky, Roll Up Your Sleeves!
>
> - Check the picture, and think, "What would make sense?"
> - Use what's happening in the story.
> - Look through the WHOLE word, part by part.
> - Look for a word inside a word.
> - Don't give up! Try something! Take a guess.
> - Reread and ask, "Does that sound right?"
> - Use vowel teams, and ask, "Would a different sound help?"
> - Don't just SAY the words, figure out what they MEAN too!

Ask questions to check students' comprehension.

As you read small bits of this text, you will want to be checking in with students' comprehension, especially focusing on the characters who star in the series. After the part where Julian says, "Not that way! Don't you know any other ways to take out a tooth?" you may say to your students, "Obviously, Julian is very upset. But why? Why did Julian say that? What is he thinking? Turn and talk to your partner." You might share a few examples of what students said, such as, "I heard this partnership say that they think Julian is afraid it will really hurt, that he is afraid of the pain and some bleeding. Who agrees? If you do, put your thumb on your knee!"

You may read together and pause at the top of page 49 where Julian agrees to have his father tie the thread around his tooth and ask students to predict: "What do you think is going to happen next? Think about what you know about Julian *and* what you know about his father." As they predict, they should use the information that they know from this story and other stories about the characters to help them confirm their predictions.

Last, you could ask your students to retell the final part, when Julian is in the bathroom. Have them think about what happens. Then you might say to them, "Do you remember the third thing that the father suggests? That's right, pushing it out of Julian's mouth. Is that a good idea? What does Julian think?"

As you reread this selection, you may choose lines or parts to have students reread, right there in the moment, to pick up momentum, fluency, and expression. You might say things throughout like, "Oh, let's really make Julian's voice scared. Let's reread." "Wait, that was a really long sentence. Let's reread it and make sure it sounds right and makes sense." "This is the father, so we have to sound like the father! Reread this to me and get your best, 'father face' on and make your voice sound like Julian's father." This will encourage students to not only read with more expression and better phrasing but it will also encourage more voices to read along.

AFTER READING

Ask children to share their thinking about the characters in the series, first in partnerships and then in book clubs.

After you finish the first read together, you may say to your students, "Let's talk about the relationship between Julian and his father. What do you notice about them in this story? What do you think? Turn and talk to your partner first." You may students first work in partnerships, gathering up some of their ideas about the characters and the relationship between Julian and the dad.

Because students are working together in book clubs during this unit, you might have club members seated together when prompted to turn and talk. Raise the level of what they were doing by saying, "Okay, let's meet in our book clubs and have a small conversation about what you noticed about this relationship. *Also* think about these questions: What do you know about Julian and his father, from the *other* stories? Is it the same here, or different?"

After a few minutes, share out a few ideas that students were talking about, so that others can hear the varied ideas that were generated and then say, "In our next shared reading, we will reread this part again and think about the trouble that Julian is having."

DAY TWO: Cross-Checking Sources of Information (MSV)

On this day, you'll reread both the familiar poem or song and specific sections of "My Very Strange Teeth" from *The Stories Julian Tells*, focusing on cross-checking words using all three sources of information (MSV) so that they read with accuracy. Help them use MSV to check in with their reading, both when they read accurately and when they miscue. Students need to understand that after checking their attempt they either need to make another attempt and try again, or verify that their attempt is correct and keep on reading. If you only ever model checking after an error, students may not realize that they also need to check even when they've gotten a word right. Students will end by incorporating words from the shared reading text into their word study sorts.

WARM UP: "Magic Penny" by Malvina Reynolds

Quickly reread a familiar text to build confidence and excitement and fluency.

Return to the poem or song you introduced on the first day of shared reading. Invite kids to join you once again to recite the text aloud with increasingly fluent voices. You may choose to mask a few words (or parts of words) to coach students to do some cross-checking work as a warm up for today's focus.

DAY TWO FOCUS

- ✔ Cross-checking sources of information (MSV)
- ✔ Reading for comprehension
- ✔ Rereading to better understand characters

GETTING READY

- ✔ Display a copy of the song or poem you used yesterday (see Warm Up).
- ✔ Prepare to share a chapter from the familiar text you read yesterday with students. Here we reread "My Very Strange Teeth" from *The Stories Julian Tells* (see Second Reading).
- ✔ Gather students' word sort cards for the phonics features you want to focus on (see After Reading).

SHARED READING

SECOND READING: "My Very Strange Teeth" from *The Stories Julian Tells* by Ann Cameron

Remind readers to continue using all they know to solve words and to check that they are reading with accuracy.

Your students are becoming more proficient as word solvers and will be more apt to use all three sources of information as they are reading. You will still want to give your students practice and support in reading a more difficult text and responding quickly in the moment. You might, for example, want to really work on getting your students to anticipate what the word will be, using the story and syntax to make guesses on the run. Therefore you might choose words like *mouth*, *another*, and *simple* and mask them completely. As students read and come to the unfamiliar word, see if some students say the word without hesitating. Remind your students that they should be thinking about what the words will say and be confirming it as they read. As students shout out "Mouth!" don't belabor it. Uncover it and say, "Nice reading and thinking work. Let's reread and get ready for the next one!"

As you read on in the text you may read in such a way that your voice trails off at certain words, such as *carefully*, *suddenly*, *happening*, and *shoulders*. You may choose to listen as students tackle these multisyllabic words so that you can assess how students read them and tackle them in the moment. As they read, you might say, "Wait, are you sure? How do you know? Check it all three ways! Does it make sense? Does it sound right? Does it look right?" If you find that students get stymied or hesitate to say the word accurately, you might try having your students reread from the beginning of the sentence, showing them the first part of the word. Then reveal the next part, asking them to read the two parts together and then the third part. Have students put all the parts together and then reread the sentence from the beginning, one more time checking to make sure it makes sense, sounds right, and looks right.

Many of the word-solving strategies will be used with words that students miscue on, but it is also important that they use those same strategies to check words that they got right. You might stop briefly one or two times during shared reading to ask, "Did we read that word right? How can we check?" Once the word is confirmed, continue reading on.

AFTER READING

Find words in the shared-reading text that match the work of word study and have students use those words to enhance their understanding of the phonics features.

After the reading, choose a few words to study as part of your phonics work. You may give students words from the text that match the features of phonics that students are studying in word study. Maybe you have a group of readers studying long vowels, another group on words with double consonants, and yet another group studying unusual long vowel patterns. Whatever the groups may be, have students sort and talk about these words. Have them create a couple of more words that fit with the feature that they are studying and then have them take out their word study sort and integrate the new words that they created and found. Then have students in partnerships speed sort their new and old words. Make sure that students check one another's work.

DAY THREE: Word Study—Vocabulary

On this day, you will want to talk to students about the vocabulary in the story that they are coming across. You may help students distinguish the different types of work that they might do with the different types of words. There may be words that that are new to them and that they need to learn from the context of the story, or there may be words that students know from other contexts that may be used differently in this story. Conclude by leading a discussion on the literary language, for example, exaggeration, that Ann Cameron uses.

WARM-UP: "Magic Penny" by Malvina Reynolds

Quickly reread a familiar text to build confidence and excitement and fluency.

After a third recitation of the familiar poem or song, you may return to particular lines to discuss the meaning of words or phrases. Nudge kids to think, "What does this *really* mean? What does the author want us to understand?"

THIRD READING: "My Very Strange Teeth" from *The Stories Julian Tells* by Ann Cameron

Coach students to focus on the meaning of words that they know in different ways.

Start to read the text together, having already covered the word *pliers*, which may be new to the children or it may be one they need to figure out from context. Have students describe a pair of pliers to their partner. Ask them to talk about what it looks like and what it does and give examples. If they do not know the word, have them think about what kind of word it is, what it is similar to, and what this word does. Then reveal the word and continue reading. Halfway down the first page you may stop and explain in *your* own words what pliers are. Use as many words as you can to describe it. Repeat this with other possibly unknown vocabulary words.

There may be words like *simple* or *method* that the students know in one context, but may not understand their use in this context. Keep these words unmasked. You may highlight them or place a piece of highlighter tape over them. After you read through the whole sentence you may say to your students, "What does the dad mean, 'This is a simple way'? Turn and talk. Try to explain it, without using the word *simple*. You might also describe the *opposite* way—what it is *not*—to help you." You may do this again with the word *method* or another one that you think is important for your students to think and talk about.

Last, there may be words, like *shrugged,* that the students have heard before but don't quite understand the nuanced meaning the word is expressing in this instance. You might say to your kids, "*Shrugged*. You all know what that means? Show me." If your kids do, then say, "So, why is the dad shrugging here? Let's reread it, and let's act it out. Let's shrug

DAY THREE FOCUS

✔ Reading for comprehension

✔ Studying vocabulary and words with multiple meanings

GETTING READY

✔ Display a copy of the song or poem you used yesterday (see Warm Up).

✔ Prepare to share a chapter from the familiar text you read yesterday with students. Here we reread "My Very Strange Teeth" from *The Stories Julian Tells* (see Third Reading).

✔ Cover or highlight words that you want children to word solve. We suggest *pliers*, *simple*, and *method* (see Third Reading).

SHARED READING 109

ourselves and think about why he is doing that? How is he *really* saying this part? *What* is he thinking in his head?" Choose another word to practice not only saying the word and "knowing" what it means but also being able to understand how that word conveys meaning about the character or the story.

AFTER READING

Help children notice and understand the literary language authors use to let readers know more about the characters.

After you have finished the third reading of the text, you may decide to have your students focus not on the vocabulary that they encountered, but rather on the literary language that they encountered in the text.

In this text, Ann Cameron has a few instances where Julian thinks to himself about getting his tooth pulled. In these instances, he exaggerates. You might put up under the document camera a couple of these spots where Julian says things like, "It was a lot bigger than I was—and about 20 million times bigger than my tooth" and "I was really afraid I might lose my whole head with the tooth."

You might say to your kids, "Ann Cameron's craft move is to show us what Julian is thinking in his head. She has Julian use exaggeration. He doesn't say the dog looks big, he says that it is millions times bigger. He doesn't say, 'I think it is going to hurt,' he says, 'I might lose my whole head.' Why does Ann Cameron make Julian exaggerate? Turn and talk to your partner." Have students talk first in partnerships, and then have them share out with the whole class. Make sure students understand that they can learn more about the characters by what the author has them say and think.

You might also discuss the phrase, "from the old days," on page 49 to support comprehension, prompting children to think about what the dad is saying. You might choose to study a few more idioms from another read-aloud to tackle in much the same way you did in this book. You could decide to push readers to transfer this work by asking partners to do a little search for idioms or other kinds of special language in their own books. Once children have found a few, you can share them out, allowing partners to share the definitions they have developed.

DAY FOUR: Fluency

Rereading a familiar text gives students the freedom to focus on becoming increasingly fluent. You'll aim to develop readers' pace (appropriate speed), parsing (reading in meaningful chunks), and prosody (expression). Prosody involves making sure the text sounds like natural speech. You will help your children listen to their reading to check that it makes sense and sounds right and, important for this unit, reflects the characters' feelings and personality.

WARM-UP: "Magic Penny" by Malvina Reynolds

Quickly reread a familiar song or poem placing an emphasis on the tone of the text to help readers read with greater expression.

You might choose to discuss the meaning of the poem before you begin a fourth read of the text. Prompt children to consider the feeling of the poem as well as the feeling of particular lines. Say, "How might we read this line? What feeling would we want to show here?" Then, allow students' voices to outshine your own as they read with more expression.

FOURTH READING: "My Very Strange Teeth" from *The Stories Julian Tells* by Ann Cameron

Remind students to think about how the characters are feeling and to make their voices sound like the characters.

You will want to draw attention to the text and support your readers with fluency. Because this part has quite a bit of dialogue, you may decide to work on how to read the dialogue and use the characters' voices. You can focus on intonation, but know that students may need to work on fixing up some of their phrasing and stress to deal with longer, more complex sentences.

You might say to the class, "Today, let's reread the first part of 'My Very Strange Teeth.' Let's have row one read the words the father says and row two read Julian's lines when he talks out loud. Rows three and four, you will read what Julian says when he talks to himself in his head. Are you ready to read? Use what you know about your character and then make your voice really sound like your character! Fathers, please start!" Turn to the last things that the father says at the bottom of page 47. After your students get midway down page 48, you might say to them, "Remember how the characters are feeling. Father is—what? That's right, very matter-of-fact. Pretend that you have some pliers in your hand. He might speak like this." You might overdramatize your voice while also acting out the lines. "And Julian, that's right, he's nervous and scared. So, think about how this part should sound: 'I won't feel a thing?' You have to make him

---

DAY FOUR FOCUS

✓ Reading with fluency (appropriate pacing, parsing, and prosody)

GETTING READY

✓ Display a copy of the song or poem you used yesterday (see Warm Up).

✓ Prepare to share a chapter from the familiar text you read yesterday with students. Here we reread "My Very Strange Teeth" from *The Stories Julian Tells* (see Fourth Reading).

✓ Arrange children in four rows so that each row can take a part in the story (see Fourth Reading).

SHARED READING

111

sound really worried and nervous. Show it on your face." Ask the students to reread, adding in facial expressions and gestures to help them read with greater intonation.

As students read, you might pose questions to the whole class like, "Did that sound like Julian's dad here? Or should we try it again?" and "What's a different way this could sound? Is there a different feeling? Is there another word you should stress as you read this part?"

AFTER READING

Continue to practice reading aloud and bringing characters to life.

Switch up the roles for another reading of the same section. Have row three be the father, row four be Julian when he talks out loud, and rows one and two to be Julian talking to himself in his head. Then you can hand out multiple copies of the book for groups to share. Say to the students, "Now get into your book clubs. You can decide to reread this same section or find another part of the story with lots of dialogue. Figure out who is who and perform the scene. Go ahead, *lights, camera, action*!"

DAY FIVE: Putting It All Together

Celebrate the work students have done reading and rereading the text, allowing the class to lead this final read, orchestrating all they have learned across the week. Then, consider ways you might extend the text, leading the class in a whole-group discussion, sharing questions or responses to the text,

WARM UP

Quickly reread a familiar text to support students' fluency. You may choose to reread an accountable talk chart or an anchor chart that will be useful in the discussion that will follow.

Since you are studying series books during reading workshop, you might choose to start this final read by focusing your students' attention on the things they are noticing the author do again and again across the story (and across the series).

DAY FIVE FOCUS

- ✔ Read for deeper comprehension
- ✔ Studying craft

GETTING READY

- ✔ Display familiar text for students to read fluently together. We suggest the anchor chart, "Series Readers Become Experts on Authors" (see Warm Up).
- ✔ Prepare to share a chapter from the familiar text you read yesterday with students. Here we reread "My Very Strange Teeth" from *The Stories Julian Tells* (see Final Reading).
- ✔ Keep some Post-its nearby for marking the author's craft moves (see Final Reading).

This could start with a look at the chart from reading workshop titled, "Series Readers Become Experts on Authors." You can reread the chart (or the portion of the chart that you have created thus far in the unit), reminding students that readers discover the magic the author uses to show how the character feels, to help readers know how the story should sound, to start and end stories in similar ways, and to choose words that turn simple things into extraordinary ones. You might say, "Let's take a look at this chart and remember all the strategies we know to become experts on the authors of our series books, discovering that magic that we notice again and again in books. Let's reread the chart out loud with our smoothest reading voices, scooping up the words in each line. Ready? Go!"

Series Readers Become Experts on Authors

- Study how the author SHOWS the character's feelings.
- Notice craft that teaches you how the book should sound.
- Think about how stories tend to go.
- Pay attention to the language the author uses.

FINAL READING: "My Very Strange Teeth" from *The Stories Julian Tells* by Ann Cameron

Reread the text one more time, looking for craft moves that the author uses.

After reviewing the chart, invite kids to read the text together one more time. This time, though, they will be on the lookout for the craft Ann Cameron uses. You might give children a hand signal to indicate when they notice something. You can mark these parts with Post-its so that after you read, children can easily find the parts to reference and talk about.

You might also choose to give children time to turn and talk about a part that features a lot of craft moves, such as page 48. As children chat with each other you might encourage children to discuss why the author chose a certain word or phrase. You might say, "Think about another way Ann could have written this. Then, talk about what she wants to show here. Look for ways that Ann lets you, the reader, know how the story *wants* to be read."

AFTER READING

End shared reading with a whole-class debate, asking students to take sides on a question.

Since children have collected ideas and evidence during this read, it will make perfect sense to end with a whole-class discussion. Invite your students to sit in a circle so that they can easily see each other. It might also help to put a copy (or two) of *The Stories Julian Tells* in the middle so that readers can access it as they talk. Having multiple copies of the text available, if at all possible, can be helpful.

Begin the discussion with a debatable question, such as, "Do you agree or disagree with Julian? Should he have waited for his tooth to fall out? Or should he have let his dad pull it out?"

After posing the question, you might first ask clubs to caucus to discuss their opinions in small groups. Then, either ask the class to sit in a circle or form two groups on opposite sides of the meeting area. You'll want to try to sit outside the group, so that you become the facilitator of the conversation rather than the focal point. Perhaps you will hear students say things like, "I agree with Julian because if you just wait it won't hurt as much" or "I disagree with Julian because it wouldn't really hurt anyway and at the beginning, he said he didn't want to wait" or "I agree with Julian because he got to use his tooth to make money from his friends."

You can jump in to remind children to refer to the text or to invite others into the debate. You might nudge kids to supply more reasons or to expand on their reasons with supporting details using prompts such as, "In this book . . ." or "For example . . ." You may even encourage kids to swap sides, and consider the other perspective.

To end the debate, you might have children come to a consensus or to repeat their opinion and shake hands.